Acclaim for *Circle in the Square*

D1073437

Restorative practices are "what's happening" in schools today. This book, by one of the leaders in the field, draws from real-life experience as well as the available literature. It is comprehensive but practical and readable: it includes the why, the what, and the how. Every teacher, every administrator—indeed many parents—ought to have this book.

— Howard Zehr, author of *Changing Lenses* and *The Little Book of Restorative Justice*

Nancy Riestenberg, since I have known her, has been one of the most articulate advocates of restorative justice in a variety of contexts. Her work in schools, however, is unsurpassed in providing educators with a wealth of knowledge about why and how zero tolerance policies are counterproductive. Most importantly, she is unsurpassed in giving school professionals new tools and showing them how to use them. It is this hands-on work—not more rules or even decent policy—that shows the promise in at least slowing down the school-to-jail pipeline. As a researcher/academic who simply tries to keep up with applications and evaluations of restorative justice, I believe that Nancy also offers practitioners a "new theory" of discipline and learning that they can clearly understand and apply in their efforts to create peaceful schools where children and youth can truly learn.

— Gordon Bazemore, Chair of the Department of Criminology and Criminal Justice and Director of the Community Justice Institute at Florida Atlantic University

For over a decade now, Nancy Riestenberg continues to be an innovative visionary of harm reduction, violence prevention, and youth development through restorative measures in schools.

Circle in the Square offers an insightful and practical guide to the development of restorative measures in schools in Minnesota.

I can hear Nancy's calm and reassuring voice in every page, in every story. True to the values and practice of restorative justice, Nancy also includes the voices and stories of her many colleagues in Minnesota, and beyond. In doing so, *Circle in the Square* offers Minnesota's rich and diverse experience with restorative measures to be told. It has truly been a story of collaboration and capacity building.

Of particular significance, Minnesota's collaborative journey illustrates how the use of Circles, as a restorative measure, has shifted from a disciplinary response to a pedagogical foundation.

This book offers a rich treasure of stories, insights and guidelines for practice, written with wit, wisdom and integrity. *Circle in the Square* will touch the lives of many people and will guide us in restoring safe, healthy, and wise education systems for all children.

— Brenda Morrison, author of *Restoring Safe School Communities*

Even the most cynical critics of restorative approaches in schools could not help but be moved by this book. Nancy has written a powerful and compelling combination of research, evaluation, methodology, and stories that argues for the use of Circle and other restorative processes. The stories are heartwarming and moving and demonstrate a belief that young people are capable of making good and wise choices, of contributing in genuinely useful ways, and of being kind, compassionate human beings when they are given the right processes and opportunities to deal with the issues that arise when we live in community. Reading this was like being in the room with Nancy telling these stories.

I hope this becomes compulsory reading for all educators.

— Marg Thorsborne, Restorative practitioner and trainer, Australia

Continued on page 257

CIRCLE IN THE SQUARE

Circle in the Square

• • • • • • • • • • • •

BUILDING COMMUNITY AND
REPAIRING HARM IN SCHOOL

Nancy Riestenberg

Living Justice Press
ST. PAUL, MINNESOTA

Living Justice Press
St. Paul, Minnesota 55105

*For information about permission to reproduce selections from this book,
please contact:*
Permissions, Living Justice Press, 2093 Juliet Avenue, St. Paul, MN 55105
Tel. (651) 695-1008 or contact permissions through our website:
www.livingjusticepress.org.

Library of Congress Cataloging-in-Publication Data

Riestenberg, Nancy.
   Circle in the square : building community and repairing harm in school /
   Nancy Riestenberg. — 1st ed.
      p.   cm.
   Includes bibliographical references and index.
   ISBN-13: 978-0-9721886-7-8
   ISBN-10: 0-9721886-7-3
   1. School violence—Prevention—United States. 2. School crisis
management—United States. 3. School improvement programs—United
States. 4. Restorative justice—United States. 5. Community and school—
United States. I. Title.
   LB3013.3.R52   2011
   371.19'2—dc23

                                                        2011018374

ISBN-10: 0-9721886-7-3
ISBN-13: 978-0-9721886-7-8
eBook ISBN: 978-1-937141-08-0

15 14 13 12 11   5 4 3 2 1

Copyediting by Cathy Broberg
Cover design by David Spohn
Interior design by Wendy Holdman
Printed by Sheridan Books, Ann Arbor, Michigan
on Nature's Book recycled paper

Unless otherwise indicated, photos courtesy of the author.
Many of the names in the stories have been changed to protect identities.

DEDICATION

To Bob, for encouraging the believing self;
to Jono, for making this project normal, like walking the dogs;
to Katherine, who said I should do this in the first place.

Contents

Foreword

Schools are arguably the largest youth-serving organization. Their mission is to provide the academic knowledge every student needs to graduate. But their mission also includes helping students manage their own behavior and become positively contributing members of the larger school community. Schools may not be able to do a lot about all the adverse experiences that students start school clothed in or are further burdened with from outside of school as each year moves along. But they can establish an environment that welcomes all students, supports them to do their best learning, and holds them to clear expectations of behavior once they enter school doors.

School staff also knows that what happens outside of school can and often does affect what happens in school. The staff need to be prepared, therefore, to address off-campus problems that affect school learning. This is why the philosophy and practice of restorative justice or restorative measures are so beneficial for schools. They help to keep students in school and, when a student is suspended, to reconnect after the suspension period. A restorative approach provides a way to build community, while also intervening with problems in ways that can be transformative for all involved. Restorative approaches help to shift the dominant social norms from "power over" to "power with," talking "with" instead of talking "at," and "we centered" instead of "I centered."

Along with restorative approaches, unifying messages can also help to shift social norms from problematic to helpful. When I worked as the violence prevention consultant for a statewide violence prevention campaign in Minnesota, "You're the One Who Can Make the Peace," one of the best parts was reviewing the applications of those nominated as "peacemakers of the month." Statewide, young people and adults were encouraged to tell their stories of small and large actions that demonstrated they'd done something to help make the peace. In addition to naming monthly winners, we selected one annual winner.

The power of restorative approaches and the importance of building on strengths is evident in the example of a student named Tara Theilman. In 2000, Tara jumped out as a peacemaker, but her journey there was far from easy. In middle school, she wanted to be a peer mediator. At that time in her school, students like Tara with physical and learning disabilities and a history of behavioral and social problems weren't selected to be trained as peer mediators. Fortunately for Tara, all that changed, and she had the opportunity to be trained over one summer.

The following fall, with the well-documented protective factors of feeling more competent from her training, a sense of having something to contribute, and a caring connection with a few key staff, Tara faced a sizable challenge to her progress when she was nominated for homecoming royalty. All nominated homecoming royalty were to walk in front of the entire student body. While this was usually considered an honor, Tara and others knew that she'd been selected as a cruel joke.

Tara could have become a statistic—a student who had been picked on and had picked on others. Now publically degraded, she had reason to be very angry and to take her anger out on the student body. She had access to a weapon. Fortunately for all, Tara's new skills and protective factors led her to use a very different kind of weapon. In all the assessments of Tara's problems, most had missed considering her strengths. Tara was gifted at writing songs. This—what some have called "weapons of construction versus weapons of destruction"—is what Tara decided to present at the talent portion of the assembly. She sang a song she wrote, "Take Me as I Am."

Some students still heckled her, some shed empathetic tears, and some apologized. But their responses were not as important to her as her decision to do what she did and her strength to carry it through. She felt great and eventually became our peacemaker of the year.

Years later, Tara told me she wound up at a small community college, and one of her tormentors was there too. Again, she met the challenge face-to-face: they had what this book refers to as a "restorative chat." The outcome for Tara was the reaffirmation that she could make the right choice, face an adversary, and attempt to "make the peace" through restorative measures.

Nancy Riestenberg's book is ripe with stories such as this one. The stories bring to life the theories of restorative justice and, along the way, they touch readers' hearts and imaginations. This book is a much needed tool to help stimulate creative thinking. It challenges the mind-set of "that's just the way we do things." And it really helps readers think about the importance of responding to harms not just in tougher ways but also in smarter ways and of facilitating among young people the possibility of "doing the right thing."

Cordelia Anderson, MA
25 April 2011

Acknowledgments

I want to thank the people who have made this book possible: Denise Breton, Mary Joy Breton, and Loretta Draths, who are Living Justice Press. Denise's unalloyed optimism and Mary Joy's quiet encouragement were like oasis water as I wandered the desert in search of a book. Kay Pranis served, as she always has for me, as the wise guide who can provide insight and direction with the ease of breathing. Thank you to Bob Cowgill and Cindy Zwicky, who helped me clarify my purpose, and to the readers: Cordelia Anderson, Stephanie Autumn, Jonathan Cowgill, Gail Hudson, Jon Kidde, Laurel Lein, Bondo Nyembwe, Jim Radde, Ora Schub, and Cindy Zwicky.

Everything I know about restorative justice (RJ), I learned from the restorative justice community, a community that spans county lines and national borders. I quote many of these professionals and community members from conversations and correspondence I have had with them over the years. I want to name in particular some of my Minnesota partners, people with whom I have had the privilege to work, to plan, and to learn. First, my first and best mentor, Cordelia Anderson, showed me that the main part of teaching lies in the listening. I have had the privilege to work with wonderful public servants, often under the radar and seldom acknowledged: Jeri Boisvert, Mary Ellison, Greg Herzog, and the folks at the Office of Justice Programs at the Minnesota Department of Public Safety. At the Minnesota Department of Corrections, Kay Pranis, Tim Hansen, and Paula Schaefer. Susan L. Stacey taught me that writing a curriculum could be fun, like making a quilt.

I want to thank the people at the county courts, prosecutors' offices, probation, and law enforcement who tested, tried, and refined restorative practices, often in spite of the skeptics around them, especially Don Belmont, Maureen Farrell, Stephanie Haider, Sharon Hendricks, Dave Hines, Don Johnson, Julie Marthaler, Carolyn McCloud, Joyce Packerd, Paul Schnell, Judy Schotzko, Amanda Sieling, and Jill Winger. Equally courageous and creative are the community partners; among so many, I note: Ali Anfinson, Terry Anfinson, Stephanie Autumn, Marlin Farley, Linda Flanders, Jean Greenwood, Penelope Harley, Qarmar Ibrahim, Jodelle Ista, Frank Jewel, Alice Lynch, Ali Musse, Jim Radde, Oscar Reed, Gwen Chandler Rhivers, Annie Warner Roberts, Mary Skillings, Laurie Vilas, JoAnn Ward, and Jamie Williams.

I am most grateful for the educators who use restorative measures, because they juggle so much with little recognition, but they find the time to imagine and the ways to implement, evaluate, and practice: Char Bentaas, Julie Young Burns, Karen Dahl, Carol Goodemann, Kathy Levine, Marion London, Linda Lucero, Dr. Dee Lundell, Brenda Romereim, Angela Wilcox, Julie Johnson-Willborg. I especially thank the In-School Behavior Intervention grantees: Mercy Adams, Wendy Biallas, Christopher Erickson, Stephen Hodder, Lucy Kapp, Carol Larsen, Jack Mangen, Mary Beth Neal, Paula Perdoni, Stacey Elliott Sarff, Cindy Skalsky, Sarah Snapp, Michael Stanefski, Mary Leadem Ticiu, Christa Treichel, Toni Williams, and Cindy Zwicky, and all the June Seminar faculty and participants.

Thank you to all the people who showed the way by first trying restorative justice, especially Darrol Bussler and Mary and Don Steufert. I also remember those who have passed: Joe Pavkovich, Chuck Robertson Jr., and Carol Annie Sullivan.

Finally, I want to acknowledge my colleagues at the Minnesota Department of Education, the Safe and Healthy Learners Team, and particularly my boss, Carol Thomas. They are all exceptional public servants who work for and with the communities of Minnesota.

A Note about Minnesota

Minnesota, home to the headwaters of the Mississippi, has a population of 5.2 million people. Its almost 900,000 public school students—kindergarten to grade 12—attend school in 350 school districts and 154 public charter schools. The student populations consist of 75 percent European American, 10 percent African American, 6 percent Asian American, 7 percent Hispanic, and 2 percent American Indian.

These categories include long-term residents, migrants, and, except for American Indians, immigrants. The largest recent immigrant groups to settle in Minnesota include the Hmong (the hill people of Laos and Cambodia), the Somali (the West Bank in Minneapolis has the largest urban Somali population outside of Mogadishu), Chicanos and other Spanish speakers, and people from the former Soviet Union. During the past two years, Minnesota has seen an influx of Karen, Chin, and Karenni people from Myanmar (Burma), Iraqis, and people from Bhutan in South Asia.

Eleven American Indian Nations are land based in Minnesota. The Dakota (sometimes called the Sioux) and the Anishinabe or Ojibwe (sometimes called the Chippewa) Peoples are the Original Peoples rooted in this region. The Ho-Chunk have also resided in this region. Minneapolis has one of the largest urban American Indian populations in the United States. Residents and citizens come from many American Indian Nations. The Tribal Nations in Minnesota have gone on record as preferring "American Indian" as the general term for the Indigenous Peoples of the state. People quoted in this book also use the terms "Indigenous Peoples" and "First Nations."

CIRCLE IN THE SQUARE

Introduction

For the past seventeen years, I have worked as the violence prevention specialist for the Minnesota Department of Education
in the Safe and Healthy Learners Unit. Part of my job has been to
help school districts implement prevention education and other
programs to improve the school climate. Many of these school
districts received grant funds to do this work. In 1998, I was as-
signed the job of providing technical assistance for the In-School
Behavior Intervention Grants. Four school districts received
funds to use restorative practices and then evaluate their use.

The outcomes were promising. The schools began using
Circles as a discipline process when rules were violated and as
a means of repairing harm. They also held regular community-
building Circles in the classroom. As these practices grew, both
out-of-school suspensions and behavior referrals to the principal's office went down. It was early evidence that using restorative justice principles and practices in school could help prevent
harm in a school and reduce violent behavior.

Part of grant management involves collecting both quantita-
tive (numbers) and qualitative (stories) data. Although the lower
number of suspensions and discipline referrals for schools in the
grant program clearly indicated positive changes, it was the stories that fleshed out how these changes were happening. One
of the stories submitted in a grant report described an incident
involving four third-grade boys.

Racial Harassment

"A third-grade boy made a derogatory comment to three other boys about their race. The restorative justice planner facilitated a Circle of understanding. Through the Circle process, the victims explained what the comment reminded them of. One said it reminded him of an uncle being shot by a White man who called him the same name as he was shooting him. Another said the comment reminded him of a movie that has 'those people dressed in white doing mean things to us.' Another victim said, 'It hurt my heart badly and I need to do something about it.' The offender/ applicant explained that he then understood that what he said was wrong. The students became friends and play together daily."[1]

I was impressed that the boys in the report could speak so directly about their feelings and experiences on this painful incident. I have asked many adults what they would want from someone who made derogatory remarks about them. They have replied: "to not say it again," "to apologize," "to make sure that others don't talk that way," and "to be respectful in the future." These three young boys did not want their classmate to be suspended, though this was the consequence for racially derogatory language in the school's student handbook. Instead, they wanted the boy to be their friend. A friend is respectful and does not say mean things. When he does say something mean, he apologizes in word or action, and he sticks up for you with others. The teacher who facilitated that Circle reported that two of the three students harmed as well as the boy who made the comment were in her sixth-grade class three years later. The boys were still friends. The teacher said the Circle/conference was "like magic."

Few things in life can truly be called magic. When you look closely or know where to look, you realize that the trick—the coin disappearing from the hand and reappearing behind the ear—is actually the "magic" of practice. The magician has worked the coin over and over in his or her hand until it "disappears."

Likewise, a conversation such as the boys had about race is born of practice, which is what enabled these boys to have such a successful and healing conversation. In the particular school that the boys attended, they held a morning Circle each day. Here the students practiced telling their stories about simple things, such as "What is your favorite ice cream?" or "What kind of pet would you like to have and why?" or "Describe a time when you were surprised. Where were you? What happened? How did you feel?" They practiced waiting their turn and speaking only when they had the Circle's "talking piece." They practiced listening a lot, as only one person can have the talking piece at a time. They experienced respect, equality, and care.

Human beings are hardwired to be in relationships, and we are hardwired to learn. Either we offer our children healthy, good relationships and then teach topics that will help them have their own healthy relationships, or they will seek relationships with other adults or youth—healthy and caring or not—and learn perhaps more painful, less life-affirming lessons. I am primarily concerned with the safe and healthy development of youth. I believe that if students are safe and healthy, they will learn.

Restorative justice is a set of principles and practices that sees crime and harm as violations of people and relationships. To paraphrase Howard Zehr, author of *The Little Book of Restorative Justice*, instead of asking the questions, "What was the rule? Who broke it? What is the consequence per the student handbook?" a restorative school's students and staff ask instead, "What was the harm? Who are all the people affected by it? What needs to be done to repair the harm and set things right, so everyone can get back to learning?"[2]

Restorative measures in schools build community, civic engagement, and relationships. These practices provide structure to problem solving. In a restorative school, people who harm others are held accountable to the person they hurt as well as to the school community, not just to a student handbook. Students are actively involved in fixing the problems they make. A restorative school is intentional and transparent in providing support to the person harmed as well as to the student who caused harm. A restorative school uses face-to-face communication and problem solving. It involves the community in making decisions. A restorative school looks for the teachable moment, especially when rules have been violated.

Applied in schools, the principles of restorative justice provide adults and children with processes, like the Circle process, for holding students accountable for rule violations, such as fights, bullying, and, in the case of the four boys, "derogatory comments about their race." But the Circle process and the principles of restorative justice offer more than this. If the Circle is used only to repair harm, then this simple yet profound communication process becomes associated with frustration, anger, and shame. By contrast, if Circles are also used to build relationships and community, then, when you have to use Circle to mend harms, the really hard conversations can look like magic. As with most things, the magic is in the practice. Clarity and reconciliation come as a result of practicing the Circle process.

For restorative measures to be really effective, they cannot be just another process to use when students get into trouble. Rather, they must become a regular part of the classroom experience and integrated into school policy and practice. Belinda Hopkins, author of *Just Schools*, says, "Restorative justice is driven by a set of values and an ethos that emphasizes trust, mutual respect, and tolerance. It also acknowledges the importance of human feelings, needs, and rights. This value base and ethos needs to underpin behavior and the various applications of restorative skills."[3]

Sometimes I think that when we as human beings are faced with seemingly hopeless problems, we respond from a lack of imagination. We do the same things we have done before, even if that response didn't really work. In the moment, we have trouble thinking of a new way of responding. Imagination can bump us out of ruts. Drawing on what we know, imagination twists and turns our knowledge into new and different shapes, forming new connections. To engage our imagination, we have to fill up with a wide variety of stories, pictures, knowledge, and experiences.

For over fourteen years, a variety of Minnesota educators, community members, and law enforcement officials have been trying out the principles of restorative justice. Their goal has been to make discipline in school a teachable moment, so that conflicts and harms become opportunities to guide and to teach—not to punish and separate. Their creativity has taken many shapes. And this decade of work has produced some profound individual stories as well as promising statistics and practices.

This book describes how these schools have been applying restorative principles. Because Circles are so adaptable not only to repairing harm but even more to preventing it, I will also describe the elements of the Circle process and its uses in educational settings. In addition to repairing harm, Circles serve to develop relationships, to build a sense of community, and, in fact, to teach any topic. They can be an effective alternative to suspension and can be used to create safe learning environments, which contribute to academic achievement. The stories and case studies that follow have been gleaned from my work with teachers, principals, behavior specialists, and school liaison officers. In sharing them, I hope to stir your imagination to develop a restorative context and community in your own school— or anywhere that children and youth gather.

CHAPTER 1

Harm in Schools

No one gets up in the morning feeling perfectly safe, well fed, rested, loved, getting As and Bs in most classes and says, "I think I will start a fight today. Yeah, in the hallway, I will shove somebody down and hit them." Rather, a fight comes out of a context. Understanding that context is part of exploring the harm and who was affected by it. Over the years, I have worked with parents and educators, as well as with my own children, to explore the story behind the harm. In this chapter, I will discuss four composite situations, based on real incidents with names changed, to illustrate "the harm."

Situation 1

During the last recess of the day, a fifth-grade girl, Amy, goes down the slide to the sand below and brushes against another girl, Dominique. Dominique turns around and pushes Amy to the ground and starts hitting her. Amy hits back. Another girl pulls Dominique away just as the teacher rushes to the slide. He walks both girls to the office. The rule violation: fighting and fighting back.

What was the harm? The fight, certainly, but to understand the fight, one has to go back to the Saturday before, when Dominique sat for hours getting her hair braided in cornrows. Her hair seemed unruly to her, and she had saved her money to pay her older cousin to braid her hair. It took a long time and it hurt sometimes, but her mom was happy with the result, as was Dominique. On Monday morning, however, Amy started to make jokes about Dominique's hair. Other girls—girls whose hair was mainly straight or short—joined in. This continued off and on all day. At one point, the teacher heard a remark and told Sophie, the girl who said it, that her remark was mean and not to repeat it. Sophie was the only one who stopped making remarks. Whenever the other students stopped teasing, Amy took up the charge. A fight had been brewing all day. Amy's brush up against Dominique coming off the slide was the trigger.

Amy was a mostly pleasant, smart girl, and she had a group of friends in the class who were all from the same neighborhood. Lately, she had found that she had a wit and could make her friends laugh and that felt good. This Monday, there was Dominique, who always smiled, with her new hair. One remark got a snicker. Another one a good laugh. Dominique smiled and took her seat. More one-liners came—in the hall as they passed to art class and then again down to recess. Others joined in—one joke after another about corn and planting and weeding and watering and picking ears of corn. Amy felt clever, her friends laughed, and then they said things that made her laugh. She did not care to notice that by the afternoon Dominique was not smiling. The teacher said something to Sophie, but Amy didn't think it was a big deal. She was just being funny. Nobody said that it wasn't funny. Kids either laughed or they turned away.

Amy did not see the push coming; she had just gotten off the slide. She was even more surprised at the hit in the side of her head. She kicked back with her feet and balled up on the ground. What in the world was going on?

Everyone saw the fight. Everyone liked the two girls. Some of the girls felt guilty for their behavior, but the school treated the incident like a fight, not as bullying and a fight. Because kids had not tried to stop the talk in the morning, they felt guilty, all the more so when both girls were suspended. In addition, because Dominique had started the fight, she experienced extra consequences. This included being barred from the class field trip, which the class had been planning all year. That didn't seem fair and some of the students were angry with the principal. The parents who chaperoned the field trip had their own side conversations about everything. Amy's mom felt terrible, seeing Dominique stay as everyone left for the field trip bus.

Neither the teacher nor the chaperones thought the suspension from the field trip was fair, but district policy called for the extra punishment. Even though the rules had been upheld, the harm was only partially addressed. The principal wisely brought the girls and their parents together after the suspension to try to resolve the underlying issues through mediation. But the role of the classmates in the incident was not considered, nor were they invited to share their feelings about the harm. Nobody involved except Dominique had ever had their hair braided into cornrows.

Amy's need to belong and Dominique's need to feel attractive—both needs played into this situation. Although both needs are legitimate, the behavior of the girls was not legitimate; it was harmful. Both girls had a story to tell, and putting the two together did provide a more detailed picture of that Monday's events. But to make a complete picture, all the students in the class would need to add their story, since many people made choices either to hurt or to say nothing. Indeed, even the cousin who braided Dominique's hair had a part of the story to share.

In her book on raising adolescent girls, *Queen Bees and Wannabes: Helping Your Daughter Survive Cliques, Gossip, Boyfriends, and Other Realities of Adolescence*, Rosalind Wiseman describes a classroom conversation in which African American girls share their feelings and experiences with hair:

"I have to sit for an hour every morning while my mother yanks my hair."

"They braid (my hair) so tight I get a really bad headache."

"I hate having to do my hair! I wish it were softer!"

Wiseman notes, "Many women who aren't Black have no idea how important the issue of 'good' and 'bad' hair is in the Black community."[1]

The policy of the district directed the principal's options, but the complexity of the harm was beyond the ken of the rules. Dominique was first a victim; by the rules, though, she was the main perpetrator. Amy was a perpetrator and a victim, but the rules could not distinguish between the pain of hurtful words and a fight. The larger contexts of culture, race, and adolescent development are not outlined in a student handbook. The consequences, based in punishment, were not satisfying, fair, or complete for anyone.

To understand how restorative principles can be used to build community and to create a safe academic and emotional environment in a classroom, it helps to review these principles from the broadest level: the paradigm level. How we conceive of harms, conflicts, and infractions directly affects how we address crime, rule violations, wrongdoing, and harm.

Restorative justice offers a paradigm shift in the way we think of crime or breaking rules. Its principles teach us to think not only about the offender but also about the victim; not only about the court but also about the community; not only about the law that was broken but also about the impact of its breaking on people. The shift is from rules to relationships.

Schools do not have laws; they have rules that guide the health and safety of students and staff. These rules exist to ensure a disciplined learning environment. But the words "laws" and "rules" have a narrower meaning than is useful in discussing what happens among people when laws are broken or rules violated. Many use the word "harm" to capture a fuller sense of what happens when rules are broken. Understanding harm in a school context is essential if we are to create safe, disciplined, and healthy learning environments.

In *Restorative Measures: Respecting Everyone's Ability to Resolve Problems*, prevention education expert Cordelia Anderson defines restorative justice in a school setting:

Restorative measures represent a philosophy and a process that acknowledge that when a person does harm, it affects the person(s) they hurt, the community, and themselves. When using restorative measures, an attempt is made to repair the harm caused by one person to another and to the community, so that order is restored for everyone. By applying restorative measures in schools, school personnel have another tool to use with children and youth to repair harm and teach problem-solving skills.[2]

In a school, the student handbook sets forth the rules that the students must follow and then prescribes the consequences for breaking the rules. But to talk only about breaking rules provides a limited picture of what occurs when things go wrong. Anderson chose the word "harm" to get closer to the spirit of the phrase used by restorative justice pioneer Howard Zehr: "Crime is a violation of people and interpersonal relationships."[3] Violations of people and relationships that do not rise to the level of breaking a rule occur every day, but these violations can nonetheless cause pain and misery—harm.

In the case of Amy and Dominique, what started out as jokes escalated into teasing. Racial differences were a clear component. As the day when on, the teasing turned into taunting and bullying, which finally ended in the fight. In this instance, the fight and the people affected by it—the students, their family members, the teacher—were connected to one classroom. Yet harm can also have an impact on a larger community.

Situation 2

On the second floor of an elementary school are five classrooms; four are filled with second graders. In the fifth is a sixth-grade class. One day after recess, a fight breaks out between four sixth-grade girls in the hallway. At the same time, second graders are returning from art class. The floors of the hallway are wood, which amplify the sound of the fight. The four girls are pushing, shoving, and yelling racist slurs. Two teachers step in to stop the fighting. One of them trips over his own feet and falls down.

The rule violation is fighting. The consequence per the student handbook is a three-day suspension for the two girls who started the fight and a two-day suspension for the girls who responded.

But the harm? All those second graders saw or at least heard the fight. They saw or heard that a teacher—a teacher!—fell down. They heard the nasty language and felt its emotional power. For some of them, this may have reminded them of when they were in a fight or perhaps when they heard a fight between parents, out on the street, or in a refugee camp. For others, this may have been an entirely new experience. Or it may have been like what they had seen in the media. Many of the second graders went home and told their family members about the experience. Parents may have questioned why in the world they sent their child to that school. The principal, well aware of how a story about a fight in the hallway might play in the home, was concerned about the school's reputation—on top of her concerns for the girls, their teachers (one of whom had a sore knee), the rest of the staff (can't he control this school?), and, of course, the second graders. The teachers who intervened were hurt as well. One of them was hurt physically. The other was hurt emotionally: those were his sixth graders, and he thought the class was beginning to gel.

And what was going on with the girls? Had they each had enough with the others' mean-girl behavior? Had there been bullying on the playground or exclusion in the classroom that the teacher should have seen but missed? Were class differences or culture differences too confusing and too threatening? Was a grandma sick, or was there yet another fight in the house last night? Were they worried that a parent was going to move out? Perhaps the loss of a friend loomed as the biggest crisis in the entire world?

Details need to be discussed to identify the harm and to determine how to set things right. In this instance, the girls met face-to-face after their suspensions, talked through the issues surrounding the fight, and decided that they needed to apologize to the second graders and the teachers. Together, the four of them went to each classroom and explained themselves. Hopefully, the second graders decided to give the sixth graders the benefit of the doubt. Hopefully, the second graders told their parents about the visit by the sixth-grade girls.

Situation 3

Beyond school walls, events within a community can affect the people within a school, like the ripples from a stone dropped in a pond.

One day in January, the high school principal came into the history class taught by a substitute that day and said that the regular teacher, Mr. Orland, was not going to be returning. The teacher was on administrative leave. The principal could not talk about Mr. Orland, but he was willing to answer any other questions the students had.

The students heard rumors that Mr. Orland had pushed a desk at a student and yelled at him because the student had been mouthing off and being disrespectful. That is why Mr. Orland was gone—for threatening a student.

What was the harm? Threatening a student by shoving a table at him is inappropriate and perhaps illegal behavior. Certainly, the parents of the boy would be concerned about the safety of their child. The school was following the district's requirement to investigate Mr. Orland's behavior. How does a well-liked, successful, fifteen-year veteran teacher do such a thing?

I do not know either the student or the teacher involved with this incident, but I do know the larger context of that school year. In the fall, two students of the school had died. One died in a traffic accident and the other had been murdered at a community center. One of the boys had been a student in the class with Mr. Orland and with the student who was threatened. Were both the teacher and the student expressing—unfortunately, in a harmful way—grief, anger, fear, or sadness?

And what about the students who remained in the classroom with the offer of answers from the principal who, due to data privacy, rightly could give none? What were they to make of this year—the deaths, the reactions of their peers and the adults in the school, and now the disappearance of a popular teacher? An administrative leave or a suspension does not adequately address any of these questions.

Situation 4

Finally, there is the complexity of cyber-bullying. Consider the following situation.

A fight happens in the hallway between two girls, Lee and Kari. Both are on the volleyball team. Lee thinks Kari is behind the Facebook posting of an unflattering photo of Lee with the tag of "Ho—will do anything for you!" The photo has been seen by all the volleyball team members, and by most of the other students at school. Lee has received sexually explicit emails from as far away as Australia in response to the photo. She reported the posting to the coach, who shook his head. Then she told the principal who said, "This Facebook stuff did not happen during school hours, so I can't do anything formal about that, but I will talk with the girls." Now the volleyball team is excluding Lee—in the locker room, on the bus, and on the floor. No one will talk to her. No one will set up spikes for her.

Kari denies having anything to do with the photo, even though the picture was on her Facebook page. Kari and Lee have had the same boyfriend. Lee's mom wants to sue the coach. The other girls on the team are suspected of having egged and toilet-papered Lee's house and yard. The volleyball booster club has met with the superintendent to complain about Lee and her mom for making their girls upset "with all these allegations."

The principal suspends both girls for the fight, because the fight happened in the school during school hours.

Rules and Context

In each of these situations, the rules addressed only part of the effects of the behavior. Mostly, rules and the consequences they lay down provide direction on how to deal with the rule violator alone. Seldom do the directions deal with the concerns of the person who was hurt, much less those who witnessed a fight, those who could have stopped it, those who helped a fight happen, or those who where scared by the fight.

It's true that rules are essential; they guide us and help bring about equality and fairness. Without them, games would be chaotic, and people would get hurt more often. But people are not chess pieces. The world around us shifts, and people grow and change. I believe in rules. But, while rules are useful in pointing out when there may be harm, they should not dictate the consequences. Too many factors are involved. A one-size-fits-all response cannot address all the harms or build a positive school atmosphere.

In their positive function, rules underscore the values of the group who holds the rules. Rules should be set for this purpose; namely, to express shared values. If a school values learning and recognizes that, in order to learn, students must be in good relationships with each other and the adults who teach them, then any response to harm should focus on repairing the harm. A violation of people and relationships has occurred and calls for the repair of the relationships. "Rather than a bureaucratic perspective that simply metes out punishment for violations of the code of conduct," writes Bob Costello of the International Institute of Restorative Practices, "our focus should be on the real needs of human beings."[4]

As these stories show, harms are seldom simple or one-dimensional. The harm that one student does to another can be but one episode in a string of perpetration or victimization experiences. These experiences often stretch beyond the school to neighborhoods, homes, and the virtual world of the Internet. A 2009 study funded by the U.S. Department of Justice highlights that children are more likely to experience violence than adults. This study provides another layer of context. Among the findings:

- Sixty percent of American children were exposed to violence, crime, or abuse in their homes, schools, and communities.
- Almost 40 percent of American children were direct victims of two or more violent acts, and one in ten were victims of violence five or more times.
- Almost one in ten American children saw one family member assault another family member, and more

than 25 percent had been exposed to family violence.
during their life.

• Children exposed to violence are more likely to abuse
  drugs and alcohol; suffer from depression, anxiety,
  and post-traumatic disorder; fail or have difficulty in
  school; and become delinquent and engage in criminal
  behavior.[5]

A study of students from an urban school district who are participating in restorative conferences illustrates the various ways that
many children are victimized. The Minneapolis Public Schools
have contracted with the Minneapolis Legal Rights Center to
provide restorative conferencing for youth. The youth who come
to the Center have been transferred out of their high schools or
middle schools to smaller alternative schools because they have
committed assaults or possessed weapons. In 2010, the Legal
Rights Center surveyed thirty-two students who were referred
to them for Restorative Measures Placement to identify common traits among the youth.

The list of the common life experiences reported by the students would challenge anyone's ability to function in the world.
The experiences included the following:

• homelessness
• moving frequently
• living in a shelter
• being involved in a gang
• having mental health needs
• using alcohol or other drugs
• falling half a year behind in school credits
• experiencing the death of a friend or family member
• needing special education
• being involved in criminal court as a witness

- being on probation
- witnessing domestic abuse
- living in foster care
- being new to the school district
- living in a disruptive situation[6]

Although these challenges may exceed what most students face, it's important to recognize that all students bring all of the harms and challenges of their lives to school. These are in addition to the harms students may perpetrate on each other. These challenges need to be considered as part of the process of restoring relationships.

Institutional Harm

The harm one person does to another is interpersonal, but institutional harm is also a reality. The U.S. criminal justice system recognizes that Minnesota incarcerates a disproportionate number of youth of color compared with White youth.[7] The Minnesota Department of Education's own analysis indicates that African American/Black, Hispanic, and American Indian students are disproportionately represented in suspensions and expulsions relative to their White or Asian American peers.[8] Graduation rates reveal similar disparities. According to the Minnesota Department of Education website, in 2009, 4,105 students dropped out of school in the state. The statewide graduation rate is 74.9 percent.[9] Specific groups of students fare worse, as the chart on page 21 illustrates.

These inequities have changed little in the past decade, despite the testing required by the U.S. educational policy "No Child Left Behind" (NCLB) and concerted efforts to improve academics in schools. The achievement gap also continues to mirror these inequities. In that same period, many districts and some states broadened their "zero-tolerance" discipline policies,

2009 Four-Year High School Graduation Rates by Student Groups in Minnesota[10]			
STUDENT GROUP	RATE	STUDENT GROUP	RATE
American Indian	41.3%	Hispanic	45.2%
African American/Black	44.0%	Limited English Proficient	46.3%
White	82.4%	Asian	68.0%
Special Education	51.8%	Free/Reduced Price Lunch	54.4%

requiring expulsion not only for bringing a gun to school but also for alcohol or drug possession, writing on a desk, or talking back to a teacher. NCLB attempted to raise standards. However, merged with zero-tolerance policies, the act had the unintended outcome of creating, essentially, a school-to-prison pipeline for many marginal, special education, and minority students.[11]

Violence and Response

In my experience at the Minnesota Department of Education, the worst cases of harm in a school were two school shootings in Minnesota: at the ROCORI High School in 2003 and at the Red Lake High School in 2005. Two students died in the former school. In the latter, nine students, a teacher, and the shooter died. The shootings were eighteen months apart.

No simple Circle can address the harm, grief, pain, and anger of such events. But relationships were clearly the cornerstone of a complex and ongoing process of responding. Relationships were reinforced through rituals, such as wakes and funerals. They formed a net across the community. Youth workers at community centers provided supportive relationships. Paid professionals—therapists, psychologists, and doctors—provided relationships. And elders, grandparents, shopkeepers, aunts, uncles, friends, and cousins provided relationships as well. Even simple expressions of sympathy and the understanding that comes from common grief reminded the students and staff that others cared for them. Sympathy came from faraway strangers in the form of cards, banners, and stuffed animals. Support flowed in from all over the world, including from other communities who shared their grief: Columbine, Jonesboro, Springfield, and Pearl.

I was part of the Minnesota Department of Education team that helped those districts with recovery planning. Both schools understood that the key element for restoring the learning environment was relationships. Their recovery lay not with the metal detectors but with the staff who greeted the youth as they came through the detectors—not with the liaison officer at the door of the school, but with the local police officer who had cookies at the 10 a.m. milk break with the students. Teachers and other adults in the districts rethought the way they taught, so that they could see all the children more completely. They began to pair discipline with other interventions, because suspension alone could leave troubled youth with too much time on their hands.

Making connections with distrustful parents and community members was not a second thought but an essential act. The need for alternatives to suspension became very apparent during the recovery, as the inappropriate behaviors in the school were so often tied to grief and trauma. Sending students away from school became less and less an option, because those children needed to be seen, heard, and supported. At Red Lake High School, Circles of Power and Respect, a community-building morning advisory program, started the day. Acting on the lessons learned at these two schools is a continuous process, one that takes years.

Succeeding in school remains a consistent asset for children. It is the clearest positive indicator that youth will have good health, employment, and relationships as adults. Although we can count on the innate desire of children to learn, we must be intentional in how and what we teach. Because learning happens best in the context of good relationships, adults must be intentional about teaching relationship skills and in creating good relationships with students of all ages, nationalities, and ethnic groups. Learning can then happen more reliably for all youth and reduce the institutional harms that continue to damage the lives of so many youth of color.

A restorative school recognizes that people and their relationships with each other form the cornerstone of both safety and learning. As a result, the consequences for rule violations in a restorative school will look different from the simple suspensions, detentions, or even expulsions that commonly occur in other schools. Restorative principles and violence prevention education explain how harm is repaired and why harm should be repaired rather than punished. If we really think about this, the concept is very basic. It is something my first-grade teacher taught me.

CHAPTER 2

Restorative Measures and Violence Prevention Education

I attended a two-room schoolhouse for my first three years of primary education. I had kindergarten for a week, and then spent first, second, and third grade with Mrs. Altoff on the second floor, while the students in fourth, fifth, and sixth grade toiled with Miss Obowa down below. I belonged to a "big" class—there were six of us: two girls and four boys. Like any elementary student, I loved my first teacher, Mrs. Altoff. She was the person who opened up words and books for me, she taught me how to write, and she was a symbol of glamour with her red fingernails and her 1962 red lipstick. She was very skilled at teaching academics. Her discipline mirrored the thinking of the time, however, with an emphasis on control at all costs. Public spanking was legal and accepted, for instance. From her, I think I learned all the things one would *not* want to do to keep children compliant and at their desks.

I remember most clearly how she used art and humiliation. Each season, we would make an art project that would be posted on our personal part of the corkboard that ran as a high border around the room. The art project in winter was to make a snowman—three white circles for the body; black construction paper cutouts to make a hat, arms, eyes, and buttons; and an orange triangle for a carrot nose. These were to be up when the parents came in January for the winter parent-teacher conferences.

Tom, a nice kid but rambunctious, was always getting into

trouble for talking out of turn and moving around at the wrong time. With each infraction, Mrs. Altoff would take away a part of his snowman. By the time parent-teacher conferences came around, his bulletin board displayed a muddy pile of snow. Despite what Mrs. Altoff told us about Tom—that he was bad—we all could see that he was funny, a good kickball player, and a pretty good student. His penmanship was a little scratchy, but he could read well and he did the arithmetic.

We also knew bits and pieces of his life. His dad hit him (that was not common for every kid), and some of us knew stories of his dad's drinking. We all knew that his dad went to help when the Delaney boy died in a farm accident, caught in the automatic silage unloader. A good neighbor, Tom's dad came right over. He brought Tom, and they had to help clean up the broken body. Tom was seven at the time. We knew, because Tom told us, in detail, at recess.

From that experience, I learned that every muddy pile of snow has a story, and every student has a life that is rich and full, whether we adults know it or not. I never liked humiliation. It hurt my spirit as a student to see another student dressed down in front of others. It is one of the reasons—a very personal reason—that I am drawn to restorative measures. I know that kids need to be held accountable, but even as an elementary school student, I wanted people to leave school with their spirit intact.

Attending to the Needs of the Victim

For twelve years, I worked for the Child Sexual Abuse Prevention Education Program at the Illusion Theater in Minneapolis. The theater's seminal play on the prevention of child sexual abuse, written in 1977 and called *Touch,* used bullying as a way of helping the audience members—children and adults—understand the dynamics of child sexual abuse. Almost every child and adult

TOUCH: a child sexual abuse prevention play, 1978. Bonnie Morris, Robin Taylor, Sonny Linder, Mary Sue Moses, and Alfred Harrison. Photo courtesy Illusion Theater.

has had an experience with bullying, either as a target, as a bully, or as someone who has seen bullying—a bystander.

The play was moderated, and the moderator would lead the audience through a discussion about bullying, asking questions such as "Why do you think people bully? Have any of you been bullied? What happened? How did you feel when that happened? What can you do when you see someone being bullied?" That section of the show ended with the actors repeating quotes from victims of sexual abuse on how they felt: "When you are sexually abused, it feels like nobody likes you. You feel as if nobody cares. You want to just run away."[1]

When I first learned about restorative justice, it resonated with me because it offered students who were harmed a voice. In sexual-abuse prevention education, we adults encouraged students to "Tell, and keep telling, until someone believes you." Telling about such a personal violation as sexual abuse can be very hard for a child to do. However, in dealing with the everyday harms of the playground and the classroom in a restorative way, I could see that perhaps we could help give voice to students who had experienced any kind of victimization. We might never know the full extent of the harm, but by using a restorative response, we adults could at least lay some foundational messages: "It is not your fault that you were hurt. I am sorry that this happened to you. What do you need so you feel safe and can get back to learning?"

Likewise, I saw that this process could provide early intervention with students who caused harm. Again, the foundational messages were there: "The community needs you, but you cannot act this way. You can change your behavior. What can you do to repair the harm and make a plan to prevent this from happening again? What can you do to give back to the community, which was also harmed by your behavior?"

The restorative conference and Circle processes offer a time and space for everyone affected by any kind of harm to practice empathy—that essential element that helps people treat each other with care. The restorative process provides the stage where adults and youth can hear and take in the key messages of the *Touch* play: "It is not your fault. Tell someone what happened. If you are bullying someone, ask for help to change your behavior. Try to understand how everyone feels: bully, victim, and bystander. Act: get away, ask for help, stop hurting someone, speak up."

Exclusion and Humiliation

Dr. James Garbarino is a psychologist who studies the causes of violence in children. After the 1992 Rodney King trial in Los Angeles, I heard him speak at a conference. He analyzed the riot that broke out after the police officers who had assaulted King were acquitted. He understood it to be an act of existence in the face of exclusion. Many people in that part of LA felt excluded by mainstream culture, by politicians, and by the institutions that were supposed to protect them. The only way they could assert that they existed, he said, was through violence. At the time, I was working as the violence prevention specialist at the Department of Education. If exclusion is a potential source of violence, I thought, why are we using exclusion in an attempt to stop violence? Perhaps our responses to discipline are at odds with the outcomes we want.

But, anyone would rightly say, people who hurt others need to be held accountable. I believe that if we do not hold children and youth accountable, then we adults are being neglectful. We are ignoring our responsibilities. And we are ignoring the needs of the victim and others affected by misbehavior and violence. We adults must respond. Naturally, it is easy to be restorative with a student who is embarrassed about his or her misbehavior, apologizes almost immediately, and looks meekly at you, the kindly but firm adult. But what about the student whose face becomes implacable, looks defiant, says nothing, and acts unrepentant?

Dr. James Gilligan, a professor of clinical psychology and social policy, studies the causes of violence and hence what can prevent it. His research with men who have committed violent crimes provides much insight. He traces violent behavior to feelings of shame and humiliation:

> The purpose of violence is the wish to diminish the intensity of shame and replace it as far as possible with its opposite, pride, thus preventing the individual from being overwhelmed by the feeling of shame.[2]

While Gilligan's research describes the motivations behind the most extreme forms of violence, the description of wanting to diminish the intensity of a feeling resonates with how I know I have acted when I have felt embarrassed or shamed as well as what I have observed of other children who were humiliated. At those times, it was very hard for me to hear what anyone else was saying. If a child feels humiliated, especially in front of her peers or friends, all her energy goes into dealing with those feelings— with trying to cover them up and save face.

Psychiatrist Donald Nathanson describes four reactions to shame: attacking others, attacking self, withdrawal, and avoidance.[3] A student may become more belligerent or simply shut down when an adult calls him out in front of other students. She may start thinking "stupid, stupid, stupid!" or pretend nothing happened, even denying actions that others have seen. In any case, the student is not really hearing a word that the adult is saying. At best, the student "gets through" the situation; at worst, he lashes out. Sending a student away through suspension, detention, or other forms of exclusion only underscores these reactions; it does nothing to teach the child a different way to act.

If adults want behavior change in a student who has violated a rule or caused harm, then they need to consider these normal reactions to shame. Adults need to help children deal with their feelings, both to ensure clear thinking in the present and to avoid more inappropriate behavior as a means of "warding off feelings of humiliation" in the future.

In a restorative conference or Circle process, the community offers the offender care and concern. This helps to separate the behavior from the person. Although the offending *behavior* is named as harmful, wrong, or inappropriate, the *person* is treated as a valued member of the community. The person who has done harm has the capacity to behave differently, and the restorative process is about supporting him or her in making different choices in the future.

This support applies to the victim, too. The person who was harmed is treated as more than someone who has experienced a violation. The person harmed is looked to as someone who can help repair the harm, who has insight into the incident, who is essential to solving the problems. Because the community offers support to the victim as well, the support helps to alleviate the feelings of shame or humiliation that a victim may feel as the result of being harmed.

To the person who has done harm, the restorative process provides the consistent message: "You are important, but we cannot have this kind of behavior." To the person who was harmed, the message is "We care about you; it is not your fault that this happened." As Brenda Morrison emphatically notes in her book *Restoring Safe School Communities*, "It is the behaviour *and not the person*, that should not be condoned within the community; hence, it is the behaviour *and not the person*, that needs to be confronted by the community . . . both the victim and offender need to be involved and supported."[4]

Efforts to repair harm that draw on the student's skills underscore the distinction between the behavior and who the student is as a person—as more than a specific behavior.

Separating the Student from the Behavior

A school social worker, also an early practitioner of family group conferencing, told me about the following conference. The agreement they developed during the conference called on the student's skills to repair harm, restore good relations, and give back to the community.

A middle school boy, Kyle, made sexually explicit drawings of another boy, Pete, and his family and left them in a common area of school. The clear intent was to embarrass and hurt Pete. To make things worse, Pete's parents were talking about splitting up, and Kyle and Pete had been good friends the year before. Kyle admitted that he drew the pictures, and he agreed to a conference to repair the harm with Pete and his parents. Kyle's own parents were divorced. Kyle's mom was out of town at the time of the incident and the conference, but his dad was able to participate.

Several things came out in the conference, not the least of which was that Kyle's dad admitted that he had been absent in Kyle's life since the divorce. As a result, he took some responsibility for Kyle's actions. The agreement included Kyle's dad committing to talking with Kyle's mom, so that they could set shared expectations for Kyle. He also vowed to spend more time with Kyle. On Kyle's part, he apologized to Pete and everyone, and he said he would not do such drawings again. Another person at the conference suggested that, since he had used his talent to hurt, he should now use his talent to help. Kyle and everyone else agreed. He created several posters about bullying prevention, and he brought them along when he and the school social worker went into the elementary school classes to present lessons on bullying. He told the younger students his story and what he learned in the conference about the effects of his actions.

In this case, the consequence fit the crime. But more important, the agreement emphasized Kyle's talents and his usefulness to the community. By asking him to use his artistic skills to do good, the community clearly indicated that his bad behavior did not define who he is and that who he is can be a great asset to the community. By telling his story in the context of bullying prevention education, Kyle was able to let go of shame and make a positive contribution. Zehr describes the restorative process this way:

> "Be it a person who has been a victim, or one that has victimized others, either way both need the social support through a journey that allows each to "re-narrate our stories so that they are no longer just about shame and humiliation but ultimately about dignity and triumph."[5]

Morrison elaborates that, in addition to addressing feelings of shame, the restorative process is about the "building of pride and respect as communities and individuals work together to right wrongs while securing and nurturing the safety of the community as a whole."[6]

How many school principals have said that they must "send a message to other students" that certain behaviors are wrong and believed that the best way to send this message is to punish offending students? Restorative measures support "sending a message," but they use other means to send it.

All our adult behavior sends messages to children. I would suggest that having a seventh-grade student talk about being a bully and what he learned about how his actions affected others— peers and adults—also sends a message. I would be surprised if any student in those elementary school classes who heard Kyle thought he got off easy. I doubt any of them thought that the adults in the school were ignoring bullying or not "securing and nurturing the safety of the community."

Entitlement and Empathy

Not all students who cause harm struggle with a sense of shame or lack of self-esteem. In her book *The Bully, the Bullied and the Bystander*, Barbara Coloroso points out that some children may have "an attitude of entitlement to control, dominate, subjugate, or otherwise abuse another person; an intolerance toward differences; and a mistaken assumption that he or she has the liberty to exclude someone not deemed worthy of respect or care."[7] Some students may feel that they are smarter, sharper, wittier, richer, or more clever than others, and so they simply do what they want. Oftentimes, they do not lose friends and may not be confronted by adults about their behavior.

But just as the people in a restorative process can support a youth who feels embarrassed by his or her behavior in changing that behavior, they can also support change for a child who may be acting out of some sense of entitlement. They can offer the child an opportunity to empathize with the person who was hurt and to gain a wider perspective on his or her actions.

In her book *Building Moral Intelligence: The Seven Essential Virtues That Teach Kids to Do the Right Thing*, Michelle Borba defines "empathy" as the ability to identify with and feel another person's concerns."[8] It is the ability to "walk a mile in the other person's shoes"—to take the perspective of another and to recognize how it feels to be that person. One can teach the elements of empathy, either to imagine how someone might feel in a certain situation or to remember how you felt in a similar situation. But like the proverbial horse taken to water, it is hard to force a person to empathize.

What we can do, however, is create conditions that offer people an opportunity to empathize. With guidelines of mutual respect, a restorative process attempts to create this opportunity. Everyone has the chance to speak without interruption. Safety—emotional and physical—is a priority. And facilitators of the restorative process are equally concerned about all participants.

Howard Zehr's apt metaphor for restorative justice is "widening the lens," and it is particularly useful for children. One of the tasks of growing up is learning more about the world around you and gaining ever-wider perspectives. A restorative conference or Circle to repair harm provides the practical laboratory for practicing this developmental task, and building a capacity to empathize is integral to the "widening," as the following story illustrates.

Opportunity for Perspective

A fifteen-year-old girl was caught shoplifting in a grocery shore. She tried to walk out with several large candy bars. The county attorney referred her case to the county's restorative justice coordinator. The girl, Colleen, and her mother both agreed to participate. The charges would be removed from Colleen's record if she participated in the conference and completed the agreements that the conference participants, including herself, made. The other participants included Colleen's mother, a teacher, a friend of Colleen's, and the manager of the grocery store.

In the conference, Colleen freely admitted that she stole the candy. Colleen's family was well off financially. She did not steal the candy because she was hungry or didn't have the money to pay for it, but because she could and she thought "the store could afford it." Neither she nor her mother thought that the theft caused any real kind of harm, since the shelves were filled with candy, and "it's just candy."

The store manager then gave his perspective on candy theft. There is a cost, he explained, and the loss of revenue is then passed on to all the people who buy from the store. So, in effect, the theft of the candy was a theft not just from the store but also from all the individuals who walk in and buy milk for their children. Theft, he further pointed out, is hard on the clerks. They experience it as a personal attack when someone steals from them. It is embarrassing and distressing for them to have to confront someone. Staff feel angry that they can't just do their job nicely but have to suspect every person who comes into the store as a potential thief. "Oh," said Colleen's friend, "that's why I get watched when I walk into some stores. It's because of other people's behavior." "Possibly," said the manager.

Neither Colleen nor her mom ever considered that taking candy bars had such an impact. The conference agreement included paying the store back for the stolen bars. Further, as a means of giving back to the community, Colleen agreed to volunteer four hours every week for a month at the local food shelf. Colleen's mom said she would do the same. Colleen met all of the terms of the agreement, which also included an apology letter to the store manager and the clerks. Afterward, Colleen's mom reported to the restorative justice coordinator that Colleen now volunteers regularly at the food shelf and helps plan the school's annual food drive.

These two stories provide illustrations not just of a different kind of consequence, but also of the fact that the way we hold people accountable matters. Treating a boy with respect by allowing him to contribute, even if he has done something wrong, helps to build pride both in the individual and in the community. Offering a girl a wider perspective helps to strengthen her emotional muscle of empathy. In both instances, restorative measures convey that, even in the face of harms, we are committed to treating all people with respect, care, and support. Everyone is important. Everyone can learn. Everyone can contribute.

This response to harm also underscores that how we send the message communicates a message in itself. If we want to send a message about upholding good, respectful behavior, then using good, respectful means to send it doubles the impact. The message does not say one thing and the means another.

School Safety

The U.S. school rampage shootings of the 1990s, combined with the school shootings in Minnesota in 2003 and 2005, influenced the behaviors of school administrators and faculty all over the country in both negative and positive ways. One response of administrators was to expand zero-tolerance polices. In addition to expelling a student for gun and other weapons possession, they began expelling students for fighting, alcohol and other drug possession, and even talking back or disobeying school personnel. A different response has been to pay more attention to bullying, to strive to make schools more welcoming to all students, to build relationships between students and adults, and to become more sophisticated about assessing threats that students make.

Much of the latter work was based on a critical analysis of school shootings in the United States. The U.S. Secret Service and the U.S. Department of Education published two reports based on research on school shootings that occurred between 1974 and 2002. These reports analyzed the circumstances surrounding the shootings and provided recommendations on how to encourage school safety and more accurate threat assessments. The second publication, released in 2004, *Threat Assessment in Schools*, lists steps for creating a safe school climate. These include the following:

- emphasizing the importance of listening in schools
- adopting a strong but caring stance against the code of silence
- preventing and intervening in bullying
- involving all members of the school community in planning, creating, and sustaining a school culture of safety and respect
- developing trusting relationships between each student and at least one adult.[9]

The list emphasizes the importance of relationships. People with strong, positive relationships listen to each other. They care about each other and feel cared for. They are less likely to hurt each other. In an environment of good relationships, students feel connected to peers and to adults.

But how do you involve "all members of the school community" in this positive atmosphere? How do you include students who get into fights, who are disruptive, who steal things from teachers' desks and students' lockers, or who return to school after an extended suspension because they committed an assault? I am finding that restorative measures provide a forum for practicing all of the components listed in the *Threat Assessment in Schools* within a process of true accountability—especially with students on a bumpy path. For a restorative process to work, everyone involved must listen to each other. The process offers participants opportunities to do this. In this listening space, people show care for each other, encourage all sides of the story to come out, and break codes of silence without retaliation. Restorative measures provide an effective way for responding to bullying, because the process, when carefully applied by a trained facilitator, attends to the needs of the victim as well as the offender, both of whom need care and concern. In a restorative process, decisions are made by consensus, so all members are involved in planning and in creating an agreement.

It is hoped that by bringing together adults and students in a process that allows for equal voice and empathy, trusting relationships can develop. Youth and adults, youth and youth, and, equally important, parents and school officials can come closer in understanding each other and can begin to identify and act on common values, interests, and concerns.

In 2000, a Minnesota special education cooperative that provided services to several school districts received a grant from the U.S. Department of Education to develop a way to use Circles as part of an individualized education planning process. The title reflects the values and goals of the project: "Connecting to the Community Through Circles of Success: Building Resiliency and Preventing School Failure for Students with Disabilities." The Rum River Special Education Cooperative produced a video of interviews with students who had participated in these Circles of Success. Over and over, the students expressed how they appreciated being listened to—that "people let me talk."[10] I was struck by how profoundly ignored these students felt. If we adults hope to partner with students on the school safety issues listed in the *Threat Assessment* report, then it's critical that we address this feeling of invisibility.

Developing Protective Factors

Resiliency researchers look for elements in adolescents' lives that not only contribute to their strengths and assets but also protect them from making unhealthy choices. One of the largest such studies, *The National Longitudinal Study on Adolescent Health* (otherwise known as *Add Health*), analyzed data collected in surveys from 90,000 students across the nation as well as administrators of the schools the students attended during the 1994–95 school year. A follow-up survey was given to almost 18,000 parents and selected students in 1996. The findings indicated two broad concepts: first, family connectedness makes a difference in the lives of youth and, second, school connectedness makes a difference in the lives of youth.[11]

In schools, connections between youth and adults as well as between youth and their peers serve as protective factors for adolescent health. Students easily feel connected to school when they don't get into trouble or have conflicts with other youth. But it is more difficult for students to feel or maintain connection when they are at odds with others on a continual basis or when they are victimized and the victimization goes unaddressed.

The challenge for educators is to maintain both their "professional self," to use Forrest Gathercoal's term (author of *Judicious Discipline*), and their connection with youth. Educators must balance both even as they hold students accountable for misdeeds or harm and support those who have been harmed.[12] The challenge lies in how educators go about doing this. How can we hold students accountable and help them recover from harms in ways that do not damage but instead enhance their connectedness? Restoring good relations in meaningful ways is the key, and it is what restorative measures are designed to do.

Developing the protective factor of good relations is not, however, the guiding idea behind many disciplinary measures. Whereas school connectedness promotes student health, typical school disciplinary practices do the opposite: they rely heavily on exclusion. Yet if health is the outcome we want from an intervention, then suspensions and expulsions work against it. They are somewhat akin to the medieval practice of bleeding the patient who has a fever instead of offering fluids. Disciplining students with suspensions, detention, exclusion, and expulsion weakens any existing connections the excluded student has with adults and peers—connections that are needed in order to develop more constructive behaviors in the school setting.

Research shows that suspensions produce problematic outcomes. Suspensions lead to an increase in negative behaviors, disengagement, and dropouts. They decrease academic achievement due to lost instructional time, while they increase the opportunities for criminal activity. Suspensions are disproportionately applied to older male students, to students of color, to students of lower socioeconomic status, and to those who are identified with a disability.[13] Suspensions clearly contribute to the pipeline between school and prison.[14]

Restorative measures take a different approach. Restorative processes look not at rule violations but at how relationships have been violated. They seek to hold the youth responsible to the persons who have been harmed and/or affected, and they challenge everyone involved to focus on ways to repair the relationships. Howard Zehr notes, "Violations create obligations. The central obligation is to put right the wrong."[15] The person who did the harm, the person harmed, and the community—classmates, bystanders, staff, and family members—work together to "put right the wrong."

Healthy Youth Development

In *The Little Book of Restorative Discipline for Schools*, Lorraine Stutzman Amstutz and Judy H. Mullet provide the following principles of restorative discipline:

- Focus on relationships as central to building community.
- Focus on harm done rather than on rule-breaking.
- Give voice to the person harmed.
- Engage in collaborative problem-solving.
- Empower change and growth, and enhance responsibility.[16]

Healthy youth development studies echo these themes. Drawing on Gisela Konopka's *Requirements for Healthy Development of Adolescent Youth*, a restorative approach to discipline uses harms to give youth opportunities to develop healthy adolescent behaviors. Making mistakes is, of course, a valuable part of growing up. Every person needs to learn how to handle our own mistakes. Restorative discipline helps students turn their mistakes around, so that the rough experiences can actually promote their healthy development.

Finding ways to do this is the trick. If we look at what youth need, we can more readily integrate these elements into a restorative response to harm. Together with youth, we can use these elements to construct creative ways for everyone involved to participate in "putting right the wrong." What are some of the elements that youth need? Dr. Konopka asserts that all young people need to

- participate as citizens, as members of a household, as workers, and as responsible members of society
- gain experience in decision-making
- interact with peers and acquire a sense of belonging
- reflect on self in relation to others and discover self by looking outward as well as inward
- discuss conflicting values and formulate their own value system
- experiment with their own identity and with relationships

- try out various roles without having to commit themselves irrevocably
- develop a feeling of accountability in the context of a relationship among equals
- cultivate a capacity to enjoy life
- participate in the creative arts, learn self-expression, and communicate deeper feelings from within.[17]

Instead of using discipline situations as opportunities to develop these abilities, the prevailing approach to school discipline narrows a student's opportunities for learning and misses a vital opportunity to develop these abilities at such critical times. When a student violates a rule, adults often talk about how the student has lost privileges or the right to participate in school activities and class trips. Students often lose the right to make decisions, since the student handbook dictates both the principal's and the student's responses. In the case of suspensions, at least for a time, the student is denied the right to participate as a responsible member of the school community.

A restorative response, by contrast, works to engage the student and everyone else involved in widening the sphere of expression. Violating rules does not mean that students lose the chance for positive youth development. Konopka's list maps possibilities of what could happen in a conference or Circle as ways for youth to repair harm.

In a restorative process, for example, youth participate in the decision-making. They discuss and come to consensus about how to make amends, give back to the community, make restitution, and outline a plan for improving behavior. The participants in a restorative justice process include the person who did the harm, the person harmed, community members, families, and friends—all of whom come together to problem solve as responsible members of a community. A responsible person recognizes when she has done harm and works to repair that harm.

A responsible person offers his time, energies, knowledge, and insights to help solve a problem and create a stronger community in the process.

Howard Zehr identifies needs for victims, offenders, and community. Victims need information, truth telling, empowerment, restitution, and/or vindication. Offenders need accountability, encouragement in making personal changes, and support for integrating back into the community. Some need at least temporary restraint. The community—classmates, bystanders, staff, family members—need "attention to their concerns as victims, opportunities to build a sense of community and mutual responsibility, and encouragement to take on their obligations for the welfare of their members."[18] In other words, the community is also in need of support in developing the skills that members need to function as a community.

Regaining Power and Voice

In schools, both victims and offenders need positive interactions with peers to gain a sense of belonging, albeit for different reasons. Being a victim of harm or crime sets a person apart. Receiving messages of care and concern helps pull the victim back into the community. Being victimized can also feel disempowering. Having a chance to articulate what one needs to be safe or what restitution would be acceptable helps to increase the youth's sense of personal power. In addition, by listening to all sides and working together to make an agreement that repairs the harm, all participants have the opportunity to empathize and to develop their capacities for pro-social moral agency—to take action for the greater good.[19]

A restorative conferencing facilitator and trainer shared the following story of a middle school sexual harassment case that illustrates how participants can regain power and voice through the process.

◆ ◆ ◆ ◆

At the high school Friday night football game, two eighth-grade boys "offer medical exams" to a group of girls as they are all standing around the concession stand. They reach out and grab three girls' breasts, laugh, and run. The boys then come back and make remarks about Pap smears. The three girls laugh and run away, but later go into the restroom, followed by several other girls, where they break down and cry. But they beg their peers to say nothing—to just forget it.

One girlfriend cannot forget it, however, and on Monday she reports the incident to the principal. After meeting with the boys and the three girls who were touched, the principal contacts the community restorative justice program: the boys and the girls have agreed to meet in a restorative conference to repair the harm. Because of the seriousness of the behavior and the sexual nature of the physical contact, the principal wanted an experienced, knowledgeable facilitator to set up and run the conference. Everyone wanted the students' parents to participate as well. The principal therefore wanted someone who did not work for the school district, who would be seen as mutually partial (caring equally for all students), and who would be able to convince the parents to engage in the process.

The girls' parents readily agreed, as did one boy's parents. The other boy's parents felt that their son was being unfairly targeted. "This kind of fooling around happens all the time. It is what kids do. Why the big deal?" This was their response in the facilitator's pre-conference meeting with the second boy and his parents. Patiently, the facilitator explained the restorative process and the seriousness of the behavior. She tried to explore with them the risks and benefits of joining the conference. It was not an easy meeting. The facilitator was amazed at how dismissive the parents were of sexual harassment and assault.

In the end, everyone came to the conference, including the mother who minimized her son's behavior at the beginning of the conference. In spite of her lukewarm recognition of her son's harmful behavior, the boy admitted that what he did was wrong. Much can be read from body language. The three girls started the conference sitting slightly slumped, crossed legs and crossed arms, and heads down more than not. As the boys told their story and as the girls told their story too, the girls' heads came up, their bodies relaxed, and they began to look people full in the face. By the time they got to the stage where they were brainstorming ideas for making an agreement, the girls were providing the boys with insight and direction. "You guys will do anything anyone suggests to you, and it gets you into trouble. This didn't just happen with us, it happens with others, too. You need to start thinking before you act, and don't listen to people who want to use you to do stupid things."

Part of the conferencing agreement included the offer from the school counselor to meet with the boys weekly for a month to help them learn skills for impulse control and to evaluate how their behavior affects others—to work on empathy.

The girls moved from being victims who begged others not to say anything to young people who had a voice and who trusted their own insights enough to share them.

This story is one example of how restorative measures can help students who have been harmed regain a sense of power. Restorative measures also provide tools for students to form connections with their schools. Howard Zehr notes that "underlying this understanding [of relationships] . . . is an assumption about society: we are all interconnected."[20] With this understanding, adults can help students reconnect with each other and with the school. By focusing on relationships, restorative processes help students see how they are related. They help youth explore their options for relating differently, and they help youth learn how to relate in positive, responsible ways.

Reconnecting with Community

A special education teacher told me a story about a seventh grader who stole money from the school store. He admitted to the theft when it was discovered, and he agreed to a conference with the people his actions had most affected: the juniors who ran the school store. Instead of pushing him away, everyone pulled him in closer. The agreement was that he needed to help at the school store: taking inventory, helping stock shelves, serving as a cashier, and learning to balance the register. He did this under the direction of the two juniors who were the store managers, both of whom participated in the conference.

At the end of his agreed two-month term of working in the store at lunchtime, he met with the advisor of the junior class and reflected on his experience. During his time as a clerk, he gained knowledge in commerce and learned some social skills. He also benefited by having had something productive to do during lunch, and he developed friendships with some of the older students he worked with. These new elements in his school life led to fewer experiences of being teased, which had played a part in his illegal behavior. Finally, he had another adult checking in on him, as the advisor regularly stopped by the store. The student asked the advisor if he could stay on by helping at athletic events in the evening.

In this case, everyone affected was brought on board to help generate a restorative response to the harm. The advisor was empathetic. By participating in the conference, she showed that she understood the difference between the student's actions and who he was as a person. The school was consistent: theft must have a consequence, and students must be held genuinely accountable. The conference was committed to student self-management: it expected the student who did the harm to admit his actions and to participate actively in developing an agreement to repair the harm. And it expected the other students—whether they were victims or as affected parties—to take part in the decision-making.

The agreement was for the student to work at the school store side by side with older students as well as with an adult—the junior advisor—who thanked him for his work. This discipline served not to punish but to reconnect the student with those around him and to establish or strengthen relationships.

We cannot afford to ignore the knowledge or exclude the skills of youth, especially if they break the rules. Adults need the positive participation and cooperation of students for a school to function—if for no other reason than that students always outnumber the adults in a school. We need to develop good relationships with each other to be able to work, to be safe, and to learn.

CHAPTER 3

The Restorative School:
Reaffirming, Repairing, Rebuilding Relationships

Most people need pictures in their mind for how to do things in new or different ways. A restorative measures training group asked for some illustration of what adults might do on a day-to-day basis if they were to take a whole-school approach to applying restorative measures.

Brenda Morrison provides a clear description of the whole-school approach in her book *Restoring Safe School Communities*. She uses a variation of the public health triangle of primary (universal), secondary (focused on groups), and tertiary (specific cases) preventive practices to map a whole-school response to bullying and other harms:

- In schools, *primary* prevention practices involve the entire school community and aim at establishing an ethic as well as skills for resolving differences in respectful and caring ways.
- *Secondary* prevention practices target groups and involve them in problem solving or talking Circle practices in the classroom on a regular basis.
- *Tertiary* practices respond to specific harms and involve all those affected, including families, social workers, and others, in a face-to-face restorative justice process.[1]

Morrison summarizes the whole-school approach: The primary or universal practices—the broad base of the triangle—involve "reaffirming relationships through developing social and emotional skills." The secondary or targeted practices forming the middle of the triangle involve "repairing relationships through facilitated and supported dialogue." The tertiary or intensive practices that respond to a specific case—the small top of the triangle—involve "rebuilding relationships through intensive facilitated dialogue that includes a broad social network."[2]

The participants in this training understood the bottom of the triangle—teaching social, emotional, and conflict-resolution skills to the entire school. They could also imagine a principal calling for a conference instead of suspending a student for a rule infraction—the top of the triangle. But what might the middle look like on an everyday basis? For example, what would it look like to stand in the hall as a violence prevention practice? To illustrate this approach, I took the essence of an actual incident. First, I described a confrontational response of the teacher in the hallway to inappropriate behavior. Next, I described what a restorative response might have been instead. Then I discussed the outcomes of each intervention approach and how they affected many people in very different ways.

The Object: A Response

A teacher is walking down the hall when he sees a group of high school boys huddled around one boy who is holding a life-size rubber penis (hereafter referred to as "the object"). There is much guffawing and randy remarks, and although the bell for the next class is about to ring, no one is moving to get to class. The teacher is insulted at the sight of the object, and yells, "What is going on here? What have you got? Jared, give me that thing! This is totally inappropriate!"

Jared responds, "This is my object, and you can't take it from me. There ain't nothin' in your handbook that says I can't have this."

RESPONSIVE REGULATION
A whole school model of restorative justice

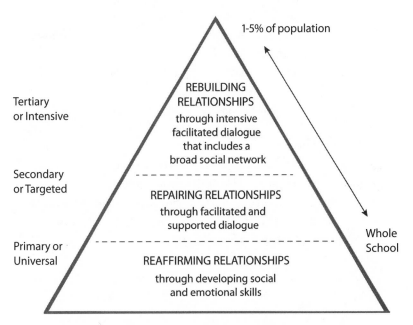

1-5% of population

Tertiary
or Intensive

REBUILDING
RELATIONSHIPS
through intensive
facilitated dialogue
that includes a
broad social network

Secondary
or Targeted

REPAIRING RELATIONSHIPS
through facilitated and
supported dialogue

Primary or
Universal

REAFFIRMING RELATIONSHIPS
through developing social
and emotional skills

Whole
School

Brenda Morrision illustrates the Whole School Approach to restorative justice, which focuses on relationships as the primary element of a safe school. Permission from Federation Press.

Students laugh, and a crowd gathers, even more than the original group. The bell has rung, but no one is going to class. The teacher tries to grab the object, Jared pulls it back, and they fall into each other. The liaison officer joins the struggle, and ten minutes later, Jared is being led in handcuffs out of the school to the police car.

Later that morning, the county prosecutor calls the principal and complains about yet another arrest from "your school." And what is wrong with "your teachers"? You would think by now they would know how to handle "your students"! He has better things to do than to have to assign a prosecutor to the "object" case. What is the juvenile court judge to make of this?

The liaison officer misses teaching his DARE (Drug Abuse Resistance Education) class, and he also misses seeing the exchange of "packages" by the lockers where the argument started, because he was dealing with the object issue.

The teacher has not been able to get much done in class the rest of the day, as he is still smarting from the fall and from the looks and remarks behind his back about "object envy." This lasts all week.

Teachers all around the school have to deal directly or indirectly with the incident, described by students as a fight, a riot, an assault, a joke, or another example of police brutality.

The mom, upon hearing that her son is in juvenile detention, calls the school and gives the principal a piece of her mind. She has been trying to keep this boy in class, and even if he did bring an object to school, couldn't it be used in health class or something?

The principal goes home at the end of the day and walks the dog for a long, long time.

The Object: Another Response

A teacher, Mr. Trevino, is walking down the hall when he sees a group of high school boys huddled around one boy who is holding a life-size rubber penis (hereafter referred to as "the object"). There is much guffawing and randy remarks, and although the bell for the next class is about to ring, no one is moving to get to class.

"What's up guys?" he asks when he sees the object. "Time to get to class: Remember our motto—lifelong learning, service to earning. Go learn!"

As the boys disperse, Mr. Trevino says quietly to Jared, "Hey, Jared, saw you in the gym yesterday. Nice dunk you made. Ah, can I talk with you a moment? Remember we can have only educational objects here at school, so let me have that object and you

*can come and pick it up from me after school. Yeah, yeah, pretty
amazing object, but not here." Jared shrugs and sheepishly hands
it over. "Thanks, and I give you permission to run to class." Jared
takes off.*

*After the last period, Jared shows up at Mr. T's room. Jared and
he have a conversation around the school's restorative questions:*

- *What happened?*

- *What were you thinking of at the time?*

- *What have you thought about since?*

- *Who has been affected by bringing that object to school?
  In what way?*

- *What do you think you need to do to make things right?*

*They both agree that the object was not an educational object
in the hallway and that he distracted other students and himself
from the task at hand: getting to class. He offered to tell the other
boys in the group that he shouldn't have brought it to school and
that he won't in the future. He also apologized to Mr. T. Mr. T
accepted his apology but offered that he wanted to talk to Jared's
mom, because he wanted to be sure that Jared was doing okay in
school. Jared agreed that she should be called and that he would
wait for her to come to school to pick up the object from Mr. T,
whenever his mom could make it. They ended the meeting with
a chat about basketball and how Jared was doing in math. Mr. T
had taught him that subject last year.*

*Mr. T called the mom, who thanked him and said, "Yes, indeed,
we will talk. I need all the dishes done tonight, and the laundry,
and the homework."*

*Mr. T told the principal, who smiled and said, "I will tell the
liaison officer. Thanks for handling this."*

*The principal told the liaison officer about the incident, and
they laughed.*

The prosecutor at the monthly community task force on gangs and drugs heard the story and said he would be sure to tell all the liaison officers in the county, in case this got to be a trend.

The judge never heard the story, as he was presiding over a felony trial.

The principal took a nice walk with his dog.

How to Stand in the Hall

Using the secondary level of restorative practices to repair relationships in a school is the place for early interventions. Some call it the "corridor conference" or the "restorative chat." Basically, the secondary level is about using respectful communication skills to address problems that might arise. In the community-policing field, they talk about livability crimes. These crimes just make life uncomfortable: public urinating, soliciting prostitution, or loitering with intent to sell or solicit drugs. If unchecked, they can lead to larger, more serious issues, but they are often seen as minor compared to burglary or aggravated assault. Community policing follows this dictum: "Fix the broken window." If you keep the property clean and fix broken windows, it is less likely that someone will set up a drug dealership in the abandoned house. If people feel as if they can walk their streets without being solicited as if they were a prostitute, then the collective strength of the community will help deter more serious crimes.

Similarly, in a school the livability crimes are not life threatening, but they do make life miserable. Running, rude language, being tardy for class, acting smart to get a laugh at someone's expense, wearing clothes that are out of the dress code, TMI (too much intimacy), or harassing language, like "that's so gay" or "you retard"—these behaviors have a negative effect on the school atmosphere. Addressing them before they become ordinary or accepted helps to prevent more serious behavior, such as a fight, ongoing bullying, or intimidation.

Keeping the air clean in a school requires constant vigilance. The way that adults respond to inappropriate behavior in the hallways is important. All the students watch to see not only *what* the adult's response might be but also *if* the adult responds at all. And, as a colleague noted, sometimes adults make the problem worse with their response.

The evaluation of the In-School Behavior Intervention grants provided evidence that primary prevention education—teaching social skills in the classroom—combined with restorative interventions in the office could reduce office referrals and out-of-school suspensions.[3] But an intermediate level of response is also needed to make a restorative school's climate hum. These are the responses that adults make in the moment, in the hallway and on the playground.

A rural school district counselor called me in the late 1990s about a weeklong series of fights that had occurred in the high school. The circumstances were culturally interesting. The Somali students involved thought that the students who had directed disrespectful words at them deserved suspension, not the students who initiated the fights that followed the words. The White principal thought the opposite. That aside, the way the adults got things under control was most illustrative. "After four or five fights over three days, the teachers came out of the rooms," my contact said, "and stood in the halls during passing time. That stopped the fighting."

Standing in the halls during passing time: it sounds like a reasonable thing to do. I remember when I was a student, my high school teachers stood out in the halls, each with their own hall manner. Mr. Schumacher called kids by the nicknames he gave them (not always appropriate by today's standards, but his wit at our expense got him our attention). Mr. Colby, Ms. Gizzelquist, and Miss Newman gathered together in a bunch in the hall, happy (no doubt) for a few moments of adult conversation. Mr. Parker and Mr. Anderson chatted across the lockers, as their rooms were next door to each other. Mrs. Sieling never came out since she was the typing teacher and had to keep the typewriters prepped. Mr. Dunwebber never came into the hall, I think, because he did not want to. Students would call him names under their breath and behind his back.

When I taught, I was always in the halls—passing. I did not have my own room, so I was forever running back to my office, an alcove one-half floor above the third floor, to get something I forgot.

Even though hall-standing during passing time was an expected duty in my high school, there were always days when Mr. Colby or Mr. Parker or Miss Newman did not appear, as they were doing some prep for the next class. Indeed, some teachers' unions negotiate hall time, arguing that the teacher needs the four minutes between classes to get ready for the next group of twenty-five to thirty-five students.

But standing in the hall has other benefits that might outweigh even prep time, as precious as that is. The director of the Kentucky School Safety Center advises schools that effective "standing in the halls" can be one of the cheapest school safety techniques. Another school safety contractor says it saves on teaching time. He once conducted a weeklong assessment on the relationship between hall passing time and student work time in the classroom. He found that teachers who stood in their doorway and greeted students took three minutes to take roll, while teachers who were at their desk as students entered the classroom took more than seven minutes to take roll. Every minute can count in a fifty-minute class period.

I am not aware of any education seminars in colleges called "how to stand in the halls," but school climate specialists and mediation trainers teach several versions of these skills, and restorative justice practitioners describe them as well.

The International Institute of Restorative Practices (IIRP) teaches school staff how to use the "Restorative Questions" that

Mr. T posed to Jared in the "object" scenario. Originally developed by restorative justice practitioners in Australia, the questions help adults "respond to challenging behavior" as well as "help those harmed by other's actions."[4] Restorative justice practitioner Marg Thorsborne, who helped to create the Australian family group conferencing model, developed the "Restorative Chat—reflect, repair, and reconnect"—-during a deep philosophical conversation at a party. She organizes the questions into three sets: those "to the wrong doer," those "to the victim," and questions "to use when stuck." Her Restorative Chat questions provide a problem-solving framework that helps students step back and engage in self-reflection. The questions also provide adults with words at a time when they most need them but may be most at a loss for what to say. Marg Thorsborne and David Vinegraad provide a longer, step-by-step description of the Restorative Chat in their *Restorative Justice Pocketbook*.[5]

The choice of words that are used are not the only important element in a restorative conversation. Adults also need to be aware of their tone of voice. How students might experience their inflection—as sarcastic or condescending, for example—when they pose the questions can be just as damaging to students as if the adult yelled. When asking the students questions, adults need to pay considerable attention not only to the questions themselves but also to how they express them and their own frame of mind at the time.

Belinda Hopkins, a pioneer in restorative approaches in the United Kingdom, stresses the importance of the questioner's intention in engaging students. In her training on using restorative questions, she coaches students, teachers, and administrators on encouraging conversations: "Ask the question, and then listen. Give sounds of encouragement, such as 'humhm,' or invite further reflection by saying, 'tell me more.'" Here is how she outlines the restorative frame of understanding that informs the questions:

- Each person's perspectives are unique and equally valued.
- Thoughts influence emotions, and emotions influence subsequent actions.
- Empathy and consideration for others motivate the conversation.
- Identifying needs comes before identifying strategies to meet these needs.
- The dialogue aims to build trust and promote empowerment.[6]

Restorative questions, posed with these themes in mind, help both the asker and the asked. Children who have been hurt and children who have done harm both need calm adults to help them sort things out. For the responding adult, being calm can be difficult in the moment, but having a game plan helps: seek insight from the student—intentionally, honestly, and with care.

The Minnesota Prevention Resource Center (MPRC), which is part of the Minnesota Institute of Public Health (MIPH), developed six prompts to help adults—school staff, family members, as well as students—address a youth who they are concerned might be using alcohol, tobacco, or other drugs (ATOD). By providing statements of care and concern combined with observations of troubling behaviors, the adult, parent, or friend can open a dialogue and offer opportunities for help. Even if the youth does not respond to the invitation to talk, at least the adult will have acknowledged the issue.

Many adults and young people do not say what they are concerned about because they fear that they may "say it wrong" or because they worry that their concerns might be none of their business. A teacher might think these kinds of issues should be left to the counselor. However, students see teachers every day, while most see a counselor only occasionally, if ever. The impact of a teacher expressing concern for a student cannot be underestimated.

MPRC/MIPH took the ATOD frame of "See It, Say It" and expanded the approach to climate issues, such as bullying, harassment, and intimidation. If a teacher sees a student behaving in ways that raise flags of concern, then the teacher voices his or her concerns to the student:

- *I care* that you feel safe in the school.
- *I see* that you are late for gym class and that you flinch around certain students.
- *I feel* uncomfortable, and I worry that you may be bullied or scared of these students or that the locker room is not safe for you.
- *I'm listening*: What do you think?
- *I want* you to be safe, and I am wondering if you might want to talk further about this, perhaps with the counselor or nurse.
- *I will go with you* if you want to talk to the counselor. You think about what you want to do, and I will check back with you in a few days.

Hopefully the student will respond to the question "What do you think?" Even if the student makes no response, though, the adult still follows through to the action-step remarks of "I want" and "I will."

"See It, Say It" provides a basic outline for having caring conversations that can "establish a personal connection and reduce defensive feelings on the parent, . . . reduce a sense of blame on the student . . . and sound less judgmental and more caring."[7] Clearly, to have this conversation, the adult needs to take the time to listen. The process involves a commitment by the adult as well. "I want" and "I need" are action steps that the student may or may not take, but the adult must follow through on his or her side of the commitment.

The Restorative Questions, the Restorative Chat, "See It, Say It," or any variation of these approaches can be put on wallet-sized cards, easily slipped into a pocket, attached to a lanyard, or put in the plastic holder that carries a staff ID. Since these questions are not only for use by adults, some schools post them on the walls around the school. Everyone learns the basic steps for discussing difficult topics, such as raising a concern that someone might be using alcohol or resolving a momentary lapse in civil language. MIPH/MPRC has videos with examples of conversations from teacher to student, youth to youth, or parent to child, along with a discussion guide. A school in Toronto, Canada, posts the IIRP questions on the walls in both French and English.

In-the-moment interventions take many forms, and guidelines on using many helpful versions are available. These in-the-moment "scripts" can augment a bullying-prevention program. They provide adults in the school with a way of responding when they see bullying or are concerned that someone is being bullied.

Barbara Coloroso notes that punishment is not useful as a response to bullying. It teaches students to be more hurtful, encourages children to be more sneaky so as not to get caught, and "degrades, humiliates and dehumanizes" the children who are bullied. Instead, she recommends that adults intervene in a non-shaming manner to problem solve and help the child with "restitution, resolution, and reconciliation."[8] The restorative chat can do just that.

Communication in Difficult Circumstances

To help adults engage in difficult conversations with more confidence, Dr. Cindy Zwicky, who works for the Minneapolis Public Schools, developed a workshop presentation on responding to bullying with a quick list of communication basics. A K–8 teacher trained in the methods of Marie Montessori, Dr. Zwicky is also a restorative justice trainer and Circle keeper. She notes first that communication is only seven percent verbal—the actual words we use. The larger portion of our communication—93 percent—is everything else: our tone of voice, our facial expressions, and our body language. All of these elements speak louder than words and can carry different cultural connotations.

Controlling our nonverbal expression can be very difficult when we confront a student who is belligerent, disrespectful, insubordinate, or mean. But, as a professional, you can keep above the fray by being aware of how you stand, how loud your voice is, and how much you are (or are not) breathing.

Values drive our actions, and we measure ourselves by how well we live up to our best values. For me, I want to go home at the end of the day believing that I upheld two things. First, if I speak, I hope to be heard. Second, I want to speak in a way that is respectful both of the person I am talking to and of myself. I don't want to feel crummy because I have been mean to someone. With that in mind, I find Zwicky's directions for respectful communication in difficult circumstances helpful.

First, she suggests, try to present a neutral or concerned facial expression. Rolling the eyes is not considered neutral. A nonsarcastic tone of voice is easier to hear, although I found that I might be genetically predisposed to such a tone. Be loud at first to catch attention, but then lower your voice for emphasis. Keep your language neutral, and state positive behavior expectations. All of this is easier if you breathe before you speak. Breathing brings much needed oxygen to the brain, gives you a second or two to think, and can be usefully dramatic.

Most important, stay on point. One topic that can catch some adults off guard are homophobic comments. If a teacher addresses a student who has just called someone or some book "gay" by saying, "Fred, we don't talk that way here," the student may seize the moment to launch a personal challenge:

Student: What's it to you? Are you gay?

Teacher: That is not the point. The point is what I heard sounded like a put-down.

Student: What! It's just a word!

Teacher: It sounded like a put-down. That is not the way we treat each other here.

Teachers may be taken aback by the question "Are you gay?" If they are gay, are they supposed to admit it? If they aren't gay, do they mention the wife and kids? Zwicky points out that the correct response in both cases is to do neither. Keep the conversation on point: the student's use of the word as a verbal put-down.

Some adults find it challenging to deal with remarks like, "He's so gay" or worse, because speaking up for gay, lesbian, bisexual, transgender, or questioning people can be seen as a political statement or a moral judgment. Other adults may not perceive the remark as being disrespectful. Some may just believe this to be the way kids talk.

But it is a moral judgment to disregard lesbian, gay, bisexual, transgender, and questioning (LGBTQ) youth and adults. Simply making the observation that "there are gay people in the world, and they should be treated with respect" does not mean that you are promoting homosexuality. This is a statement of fact under our system of democratic government, which honors human rights. The observation is akin to saying, "There are Liberian people who live in Minnesota, and they should be treated with respect." Such social and political realities are why disrespectful remarks by students need to be addressed. Adults should respond to words that are put-downs of any group, including gay, lesbian, bisexual, and transgender people. If we allow one group to be put down, then we are giving tacit approval for all put-downs. Students are waiting to see *if* adults will respond and *how* they respond.

A high school student in a focus group on school safety reported that only one teacher in her high school ever said anything when students would say, "Oh, that's so gay." As an out lesbian, she was so grateful that the teacher would immediately address the remark and the student who said it. "I shouldn't have to be the one who says to other students, 'Cut it out,' when they are being disrespectful to me and my friends all the time. I am glad I can just sit in that class and just be another student."

Solution Focus and Trauma Precautions

Another approach to mid-level and high-end interventions is "Solution-Focused Practices" (SFP), which Linda Metcalf outlines in her book *Counseling Toward Solutions*.[9] The Carver Scott Educational Cooperative, which runs an alternative learning center, trained their staff in SFP. Richard Scott was the coordinator for the grant that funded the training. He explains the two premises on which the practices are based: "Children and youth naturally want to be in relationships, and they look for positive relationships, not negative ones. They naturally want to learn." Any child's action contrary to this agenda probably has a reason behind it. Solution-Focused Practices is designed to help students explore preferred alternatives to their behavior. Adults do this by prompting students to identify their own solutions to problems through a series of questions. "Because the student chose the alternative, he is internally motivated to follow his solution," Scott noted.[10]

This process directs the adult to respond to the student and not to the rule. Scott gives the following example:

A student comes to school and class late. The rule of the school says the student is tardy and should take a blue slip down to the office to document the violation. Instead, the teacher greets the student at the door and says, "I am glad you are here. You must have had a hard time getting here—we are glad you came. Have you had breakfast yet? When you are settled, let's talk about what you missed and what you need to catch up."

At the end of the class, the teacher may say, "I need to send this blue slip down to the office because you were late, but I will make a note of the fact you are caught up in the class."[11]

In learning Solution-Focused Practices or any approach that engages the student in problem solving rather than strict enforcement of rules, teachers may be concerned that they are handing control over to the student. Scott's view is different: "It is not about teachers losing control. It is about reframing control and how teachers use their control differently."

Adults who work with students should always be respectful. As one teacher put it, "Remember, that child is someone's darling." Forrest Gathercoal says that being professional means treating all students with respect, regardless of their actions.[12] Perhaps most important, in addition to modeling respectful behavior, talking to students in a respectful way allows adults to follow the maxim "First, do no harm."

According to a report titled *Responding to Childhood Trauma: The Promise and Practice of Trauma Informed Care*, Gordon R. Hodas, MD, states that students who have experienced trauma need "unconditional respect." Adults must take care that traumatized youth not be challenged "in ways that produce shame and humiliation." One cannot know whether a child in a class has experienced trauma, so universal precautions are in order. Applying these principles universally, the report states, "has no down side, since children who have been exposed to trauma require it, and other, more fortunate children deserve and can also benefit from this fundamentally humanistic commitment."[13] Hodas elaborates,

> A humanistic approach is appropriate for all children, and is especially important for children who have been traumatized, even if they present with challenging behaviors. To possible skeptics concerned that the above approach may be "soft," we offer the reminder that positive change nearly always occurs within the context of respectful, trusting relationships. In addition, genuine respect inherently presupposes that the child is held responsible and accountable.[14]

A child who feels respected is more likely to be receptive to expectations and to being held accountable.

These are a few of the many excellent programs that are helping to advance a restorative philosophy. They are making school climates healthier and the air in the hallway safe for all. Whatever the program, consistent responses—even if all this means is that every adult will at the very least say "Language!" when disrespectful words are used—is important.[15] We would like students to respond to our observation that they are being rude or mean by saying, "Oops, you're right, Ms. Knutson, I apologize." More often than not, they won't. This doesn't mean, though, that adults should refrain from stating the obvious. We are talking not only to the student who has said something offensive but also to the bystanders. Students hear what adults say, regardless of their blank looks, lack of eye contact, or snide remarks.

It helps considerably to offer training in how to conduct problem-solving conversations. We know that if the situation warrants it, the office will engage a problem-solving process for just about anything. This gives the entire school community some confidence that everyone's ability to resolve problems will be called upon to work things out in a good way.

Peer Mediation and a Restorative Process

A parent once contacted me because she was concerned that her daughter was being pressured into participating in a conflict-resolution process that the mother did not think was appropriate. The situation was this: Alyssa had jumped Marni, the woman's daughter. Marni hit her assailant back, causing a black eye. Both ninth-grade girls were suspended. When they returned to the school, the dean suggested the two girls try to resolve their fight in a peer mediation session with an eleventh-grade mediator.

The dean knew that the physical fight came from a disagreement and that the girls would need to work things out. What he did not know—and what the mother learned from talking with Marni—was that the dispute was about a boyfriend and possible dating violence. Alyssa had shared with Marni that she and her boyfriend were fighting and that she was scared of him. Marni had betrayed Alyssa's trust by telling other girls in the school. To complicate matters, the two girls were on-again, off-again friends. Alyssa's parents wanted to have Marni arrested for assault. It seems that neither set of parents were particularly pleased with the dean's work thus far. Neither family thought their daughter should have been suspended.

Given what she knew of the situation, Marni's mother did not think it was appropriate to have an eleventh grader serve as mediator for the fight or to deal with a girl who may be in a violent relationship, not to mention her daughter who had betrayed her friend's confidence. Alyssa's parents were calling Marni's actions bullying. Students were commenting on Alyssa's situation on Facebook. Alyssa's reputation seemed ruined.

I think of communicating on a continuum: basic skills flow from one part of the line to the next in ever-increasing complexity. One end of the continuum roots communication in basic, social, and emotional skills. In their book *Positive Discipline in*

Communication Continuum

→ Listening and speaking
→ Sharing, negotiating, and problem-solving
→ Conflict resolution
→ Conflict resolution with a mediator
→ Restorative conferencing or Circles

As communication becomes more complex, the kinds of processes required to address needs for information, to problem solve, and to repair harm become more complex as well.

the Classroom, Jane Nelson, Lynn Lott, and H. Stephen Glenn identify these skills as "the ability to work with others through listening, communicating, cooperating, negotiating, sharing, and empathizing."[16] Negotiating differences that arise requires that we use simple conflict-management skills: taking turns, listening, problem solving, brainstorming solutions, evaluating choices, and then choosing a solution. If a conflict escalates or becomes more complex, disputants may need mediators to help them engage in problem-solving processes. When problems become more than a conflict—when someone has been harmed and the harm has created a power imbalance—communication must move further along the continuum to a restorative process. Each process builds on the basic communication skills, adding elements to address the increased complexity: conflicts, harms, power imbalances, multiple layers of harms, and multiple participants.

The situation in this example was complex: the fight, the betrayal, and all the underlying issues—possible dating violence, bullying behavior, the embarrassment of Facebook gossip, and parental concerns. Harms also cause power imbalances, which must be addressed skillfully. Responding to the harm in a reparative way required more controls and a larger skill set than is usually found in peer mediation.

Peer mediation is useful to address problems in the early stages of a conflict and when both participants have mostly equal power. Richard Cohen describes it this way:

> Mediation is a structured method of conflict resolution in which trained individuals (the mediators) assist people in dispute (the parties) by listening to their concerns and helping them negotiate.[17]

However, if I have been spreading mean rumors about you, acting like I am your friend one day but not talking to you the next, and getting all my friends to ignore you, then I have created a power imbalance between us, and I am engaging in behavior that intentionally hurts you. Asking you to negotiate with me does not make much sense. More elements are needed to repair the harm.

In a situation like the one I just described, a restorative process would work to establish a balance between you and me. A facilitator would take time with each participant to prepare everyone before bringing the group together. I would admit that I did something wrong. You would be asked what you needed to feel safe so that you could talk with me. Do you need, for example, the presence of family, friends, or other supporters? Everyone would choose whether to attend the conference or Circle. Everyone would agree on following specific guidelines for the meeting. Best practices in restorative justice help to "even out" power imbalances, so that all parties can work together to repair the harm and restore the community.

Bullying over time creates a large power imbalance, and peer mediation has not proven to be effective in addressing this degree of imbalance. Noted bullying researcher Ken Rigby notes, "An emerging consensus appears to be that mediation processes in dealing with bullying have quite limited applicability in schools, although they may play a part in some cases of interventions and are certainly helpful in promoting a school ethos in which bullying is less likely to occur."[18]

I am aware that many adult mediators, whether professional or those who practice out of the counselor's office at XYZ High School, have the skills and the experience to make the needed shifts and to account for power imbalances when they arise, even in the middle of a mediation. Experienced mediators move easily from negotiation to repairing harm, depending on the situation.

Bullying interventions rage from applying rules and consequences to building on shared concerns to engaging restorative measures. Any intervention will be more successful if the school has a clearly stated policy about bullying. Anti-bullying content in the school curriculum plays an important role in prevention. And devoting school time to social and emotional learning and community building pay off. They create a safer school atmosphere, provide a base of understanding and experience for handling conflicts, and, most of all, build a more effective environment for learning. Rules, peer mediation, restorative practices, and other non-punitive responses are all needed to create a safe and caring school.

One district that has used both peer mediation and restorative practices is Anoka Hennepin. Karen Dahl served as the district's student assistance coordinator and director of the peer mediation program. She set up a kind of triage to determine the response for student issues. In each school building that had peer mediation, a mediation coordinator would determine if a dispute went to peer mediators, adult mediators, or to the community agency that conducted restorative group conferencing. "The coordinators would check to see if bullying behavior was an element of the students' difficulties," she said. "If it was, peers did not handle the face-to-face meeting; an adult did. In severe situations—or if there was clear, direct harm, as in a fight—we would refer the case to Mediation Services of Hennepin County. Some staff also would conduct restorative Circles, if the situation warranted it and the policy allowed it."[19]

In the Minneapolis Public Schools, Julie Young Burns, the School Climate Coordinator, reports that "he said/she said" disputes and disputes that have gang overtones are referred to Mediation Services, a community agency. The name of the process—"restorative justice" or "mediation"—is not as important as having a trained facilitator. Facilitators need skill and experience in supporting face-to-face problem-solving processes. Such communication often reveals dynamic issues, and participants need skilled help in working through them.

A restorative process does not always proceed by the book. Cindy Skalsky, a trainer and conferencing facilitator from Fergus Falls (a central Minnesota district), told a story of two boys involved in a series of fights. By the time the case got to her, the parents of the boys were furious with each other. Each family threatened the other with retaliation, lawsuits, and assault charges. They were refusing to look at each other in the grocery store.

Skalsky began her work by holding pre-meetings to see who might be willing to come together in a restorative conference. She started with the boys. The boys both agreed that the parents would be an impediment to good communication: they could work this out themselves. So Skalsky held a conference with the boys where they discussed their differences, identified the harm they had caused, and came up with a plan to repair it. They also developed a plan to communicate all this to their parents to help diffuse the families' anger. By presenting their plan to the adults, the boys were able to help their parents save face and back down. Sometimes starting small, as in this case with a two- or three-person restorative conference, can speed up the process of addressing everyone's concerns.

My questions to educators who say, "We are restorative—we do mediation," are not about what they call the process but about what happens during it. What outcomes are hoped for? Do the participants in a face-to-face meeting seek to answer the core questions: What happened? Who was affected? What can we all do to put things right?[20]

A restorative process generally includes the following elements:

- addresses the needs of the person harmed
- expects the person or persons who have done harm to admit they did something wrong, even if both sides have been harmed and done harm
- expects that all participants will work to solve the problem
- uses consensus as the way of making decisions
- creates an agreement that outlines ways of repairing the harm(s)—a plan for changing behavior and for those who did harm to give back to the community
- creates a plan for safety and/or support for the victim(s), if needed
- creates connections to caring adults for all students who have been affected by the harm, whether victims, offenders, or bystanders.

Schools are most restorative when they engage students at every level of the whole-school triangle. You get further faster if you teach social skills to all the students, *and* expect them to use those skills themselves, *and* help them repair harms by using restorative conferences or Circles.

CHAPTER 4

Circles in Schools: The Basic Elements

When the teacher picks up the stuffed black bear—the elementary school's mascot—the children know that this is the signal to leave their work, push their chairs up tight, and sit at the meeting rug for Circle. Ms. Linda asks the students to close their eyes and breathe with her. They take eight breaths in and out. Then they open their eyes. The students read their agreements in unison:

talk when you have the bear;

listen with care;

be kind;

our stories we will find.

Since the science lesson that day was about insects, the introductory round started with, "Say your name and answer the question, if you could be a bug today, what kind of bug would you be?" Most of the students wanted to be either dragonflies or butterflies. One boy wanted to be a mosquito, because then he could bug his brother. Another wanted to be a water strider but a big one, like a jet ski. The teacher noted that no one wanted to be a cockroach! The next question was, "What kind of bug would you definitely not want to be?"

The Circle was light and whimsical—just the thing to get people ready for the math lesson. In the final round, the students "send around the compliment"—they compliment the student to their

Connections between students and students as well as between students and staff develop as participants slow down and take the time to listen in Circle. Photo by Brenda Romereim.

left. The teacher closed the Circle by asking the students to stand and touch each other toes-to-toes. She thanked them for speaking out loud or in their head. It was a good Circle, because no one fell backward touching toes, like they did the first time they tried it!

The talking or peacemaking Circle is an intentional communication process guided by a community's values. It is based in the wisdom of Indigenous Peoples. The Circle can be used to help people get to know one another, direct a meeting, teach, support someone in need, or hold someone accountable for harm or rule violations.

The shape of the Circle illustrates equality—there is no head of the line or back of the room. It also suggests joint ownership of the process. The participants sit so that everyone sees each other. That means everyone can see if two people are holding a side conversation, and everyone can hear kind, direct, or harmful words.

The shape has metaphorical meaning as well. As Indigenous people point out, the earth is a circle. Our head is a circle; there are circle shapes all over the human body as well as in plants and animals. Black Elk, *Hehaka Sapa* (1863–1950), a famous Oglala Lakota Holy Man, described the wisdom inherent in the circle:

> Everything the Power of the World does is done in a circle. The sky is round, and I have heard that the earth is round like a ball and so are all the stars. The wind, in its greatest power, whirls. Birds make their nests in circles, for theirs is the same religion as ours. The sun comes forth and goes down again in a circle. The moon does the same and both are round. Even the seasons form a great circle in their changing, and always come back again to where they were. The life of a man is a circle from childhood to childhood, and so it is with everything where power moves.[1]

But the most practical part of the Circle is its transparency. One need know only that the talking piece moves in order around the circle of participants. Any question about "when can I talk?" and "when can I listen?" is answered by the talking piece. I do not have to think, "Did I as the teacher call on that student? Is there someone I missed?" The talking piece guides the eye and the attention to each participant.

A Circle is not directed by a person who is in the role of a teacher, social worker, or administrator. Rather, it is guided by a person who assumes the role of Circle keeper. The keeper does not make decisions for the group but allows and encourages all Circle participants to work together to find their own answers. Circle decisions are made through consensus. Using the values articulated by the members, the participants develop agreements or guidelines that everyone in the Circle agrees to follow. In this way, Circles are fundamentally democratic.[2]

To be most effective in a school or youth program, the Circle should be used on a regular basis as a communication process. All students and staff come to understand the basics: the purpose of sitting so that everyone can see everyone else's face, what a centerpiece is for, and how the talking piece works. Some uses of the Circle require only a basic understanding of the process and a willingness to try it. Other uses require more skill and experience. Using the Circle process to repair harm, for example— disruption in a classroom, bullying, or a fight—requires training, practice, and mentorship for the keeper.

The Elements of Circles in Schools

The boys gather once a week for their Circle in Mr. Reed's room. They start the same way. Once everyone is seated, they stand and follow the leader going around and shaking the hand of every boy in the Circle. Seated again, they sit in silence for a minute. Then the talking piece—a large seashell someone brought from a trip to see relatives on the Gulf coast—goes around. Each boy says his name and one of the guidelines that he resonates with that day.

The co-captain, who is the Circle keeper for the session, asks for a check-in. Many boys are particularly concerned about a rumor of a fight that may take place later in the day. Others are worried about the upcoming MCA tests (Minnesota Comprehensive Assessments—state tests). When the shell comes back to him, the keeper asks for suggestions about how to deal with the fight. Several ideas are offered. A few boys know one of the possible fighters, and they are going to go sit with him at lunch. Maybe they can find out what the deal is and help him avoid trouble.

In the midst of these suggestions, one boy asks for after-school tutoring for math. Three speakers later, Mr. Reed, who is the restorative justice guide in the school, takes the shell and offers to talk with him and the math teacher. The boys end the session with one more go-round: "In one word, how was the Circle for you?" As the shell comes back to the keeper, the bell rings and, like students everywhere, they all get up and leave. Next week, during a different hour on a different day, they will do the same thing.

Circles in schools have many applications. The process certainly works well for building community, solving problems, or handling discipline situations. A number of educators have also used it to teach and organize their classes. Some just introduce the talking piece and the basic guidelines: "When you have the talking piece, you may talk, and when you don't, you may listen. Let's send this around the circle in order. Now, tell me one thing you know about the American Revolutionary War." Other teachers have found it useful, even necessary, to teach the elements of the Circle as a way to build a community of learners.

The physical elements of the Circle as a communication process include

- a circle of chairs or participants sitting on the floor in a circle
- the talking piece
- a centerpiece.
- The elements that provide the communication structure for the process include
- discussing values
- developing guidelines or common agreements
- making decisions by consensus
- honoring confidentiality
- creating a safe place
- maintaining the option to pass.

A keeper facilitates the process. When working with children and youth, adults need to consider how to discuss their mandated reporting responsibilities and their concerns for the safety of all participants. The historical Indigenous roots of the process provide a rich context for the elements and can inform how Circles are applied.

Like learning to play basketball, youth can learn about each element of the Circle either through explicit instruction or simply by practice. Here are descriptions of the basic elements of Circles. I also offer some examples of how elementary and secondary teachers, social workers, and youth workers who have become "RJ School Guides" have taught and used these elements.

How to Build a Circle

The Talking Piece

Jack came with his collection of children's books to talk with teachers and principals about using children's literature to teach values and address harm in elementary classrooms. But first, he pulled out a bleached white turkey feather. "If you are going to use Circle and restorative measures in your school," he said, "get yourself a feather. The feather provides a wonderful metaphor for students. If the tines of the feather are ruffled, and messed up"—here he ran his hand from top to bottom of the feather—"the bird cannot fly. Just like if there is hurting in a classroom or the students are not working together with their teacher, they cannot learn. But if the tines are in order, smooth, and going upward"—here he stroked the feather bottom to top—"then the bird can fly, and fly all the way from the Artic Circle to Antarctica. As the feather goes around the Circle and each of you has the chance to talk, I invite you to give the feather a stroke to smooth it out. We may put this feather back together, like we can talk and put a class back together. So if you are going to do Circles in school, I recommend that you get yourself a feather."

The basic tool of the Circle is the talking piece. The talking piece directs the conversation. When a person has the talking piece,

The talking piece is passed in order from one person to the next around a high school student Circle. Photo courtesy of St. Louis Park High School (SLPHS).

he or she may speak, hold the piece in silence, or pass it on to the next person. People speak of "respecting the talking piece." That phrase has several meanings. One is that when you don't have the talking piece, you listen. This offers simple control over the conversation. "Honor the talking piece" also means that the person holding the piece is respectful in his or her words and honest in what he or she says. "I have been in Circle," one Ojibwe keeper said, "with teens involved in gangs. And they have passed the eagle feather, because they would not lie. To speak the truth would be to admit to crimes. So they passed, out of respect."

A talking piece is much like a baton in a conductor's hand. The musicians agree to follow the baton and to work together under its control. Like the direction of the baton, the talking piece directs the group. No one has to wonder, "Should I jump in here? Can I interrupt? Do I have my hand high enough in the air?" The talking piece brings together the members of the Circle to work together in a respectful way.

Self-control, speaking respectfully, being honest: these are the components embodied in a talking piece, and they can be taught in a number of ways. One way is to simply let Circle participants

An Ojibwe Elder speaks of values as she holds an eagle feather talking piece at the Anishinabe Academy Girls Circle. Photo by Kaori Sakagami.

experience the Circle. As the piece goes around, they will see how others honor or respect the talking piece and the person who holds it. In Minnesota Ojibwe hands, the talking piece is usually an eagle feather, which is sacred in many Indigenous traditions. Respecting the talking piece when that piece is sacred to your tradition is pretty straightforward. So, too, if you understand the meaning behind the object—be it a rock from Lake Superior, Grandmother's prayer book, or a carved, ebony figure from Kenya—you naturally respond to the talking piece's use with respect.

But how does one communicate the idea of respect of an object to a group of third graders in a suburban elementary school or to a multi-aged group in the inner city after-school program? One teacher from a small town addressed the issue by having students make their own talking pieces. She brought in feathers,

The person holding the talking piece speaks, while the other Circle participants listen. Photo courtesy of St. Louis Park High School (SLPHS).

sticks, beads, shells, rocks, ribbon, yarn, and other items. With the help of a scissors, glue, or a hot glue gun, the students set out to make their own talking pieces.

The students had two tasks: to make a talking piece that could be used in the classroom and to make one to give to someone outside of the school who had taught them something. The class discussed symbolism—what colors could represent and what meaning besides being a stick an object might have. For instance, if the student learned how to fish from her grandfather, she might select a stick to represent the pole and then tie green and blue ribbons to it to represent the fish and the water.

Creating a talking piece to give away offered the class the opportunity to discuss numerous topics—the process of lifelong learning, of finding teachers in all parts of their lives, of practicing generosity, and of showing respect to people who help them. With older students, the activity can be connected to a story or novel. It can involve an essay or a research project on cultural objects and their meanings. The second talking piece can become part of the collection of talking pieces that can be displayed in the classroom and used when it is a student's turn to keep the Circle.

Another way to illustrate the symbolic meaning of the talking piece is to discuss objects that hold meaning for people. Participants in a seminar on restorative justice are sometimes asked to bring in an object that means something to them and explain it as a way of introducing themselves to the learning community. While their name tag may indicate that they are a principal or a social worker, what the participants say about their object of significance provides a broader picture of who they are. This exercise works well with young people too.

People have brought in, for example, pieces of jewelry that are valuable not for their monetary worth but for what they symbolize: the love of a life partner, the guidance of a grandmother, or the memory of a deceased friend. One person held out his police badge. He explained that it not only officially identified his office but also connected him to his family: his father, grandfather, nephews, and a niece were also police officers. Rock climbing links, water bottles, and swimming caps identify favorite activities. Stuffed animals, a lanyard made by a child at camp, or a photograph might represent the person's relationships with children or students.

Whether by making their own object or by bringing in an object and describing what it means for them to others, students learn that if they want their talking piece respected, they need to respect other talking pieces.

The Centerpiece

Even though it is not essential to the Circle process, a centerpiece can help welcome people to the process and provide a physical representation of the Circle community. A quilt that includes an

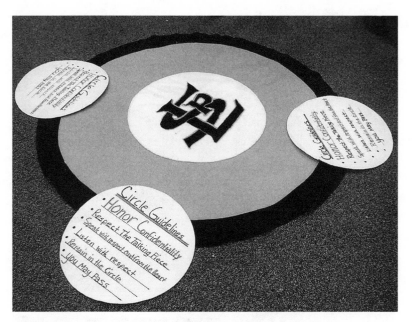

The centerpiece used for Circles at St. Louis Park High School is made with the school district logo and the school colors. Photo courtesy of St. Louis Park High School (SLPHS).

embroidered Hmong square, a piece of Kinte cloth, a piece of Scottish tartan, and a piece of fringed deerskin or beaded cloth, all bounded by the colors of the school, can provide an easy way for students and other Circle participants to see themselves welcomed to the Circle in the centerpiece. A centerpiece provides focus for participants. It also offers a place for participants to rest their eyes without being disrespectful to the person speaking.

One way to make a centerpiece is to simply lay a scarf or piece of cloth in the middle of the circle and invite students to place small objects of meaning on the cloth. At the end of the Circle, the piece of cloth can be rolled up and stored for the next Circle.

Creating a weaving is another idea for a centerpiece. Sarah Smith, a fourth-grade teacher, provided each student with a strip of cloth and markers. The students were asked to draw a picture

The values of the Circle can be incorporated into other classroom lessons. A third grade class made an acrostic from the value, trust. Photo by Sarah Smith.

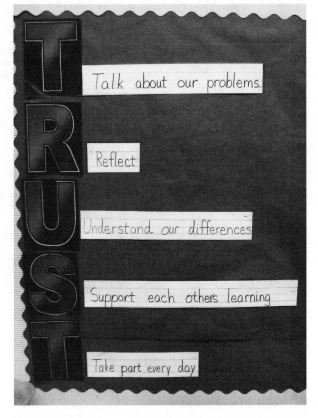

or write words that described one or two things that they valued. Or, they could draw a picture of themselves and the important people in their lives. These strips were woven together and sewn into one large piece of cloth. The class then discussed what was seen and what was hidden and how one side looked different from the other. They also talked about how these ideas of seen and hidden, similar and different factored into friendships, how people work together, inside and outside traits and strengths, and ways of getting along with each other.

Using a quilt as a centerpiece offers a symbol of community: individual pieces are stitched together and supported by a common backing. I use a white bedsheet with the red, yellow, and blue handprints of children who were part of a peacemaking retreat. It folds up quickly and washes easily. Some people use a candleholder, such as a circle of figures holding hands. Others put a bowl of water on a scarf. A vase of flowers cheers any space. For practical purposes, it helps to have a box of tissues handy.

After creating talking pieces and, as a group, chosen or created a centerpiece, the next step in building a Circle community is to discuss the values that students bring to their school, their class, and the Circle space.

Circle Values

The Circle gathered in the atrium of the school. Third-grade and eighth-grade girls had just served tea to a group of grandmothers—elders from the community. The group meets for tea, Circle, and lunch once a month. The talking piece was an eagle feather brought by one of the elders. The girls and women started the Circle by sitting in silence a moment. Then the feather circled, and everyone said her name. The feather went around again, and the girls read from laminated pieces of paper the seven Ojibwe values of their Circle: Honesty, Humility, Truth, Wisdom, Love, Respect, Bravery. Each of the elders shared a value that had directed her life and that she wanted to pass on to the girls. The elders and the girls then talked about what one of the values means to them. They closed the circle with one of the eighth-grade girls reading a passage from a book of her choice that illustrated one of the values. Then everyone ate lunch together. After lunch, the girls went back to class, and the elders returned to their homes.

Communities organize themselves according to their values. Rules, ways of acting, protocols, and etiquette make the most sense when we understand the values they represent. Some cultures expect people to look each other in the eye when they greet

Anishinabe Academy in Minneapolis invites Ojibwe Elders to their school for tea and Circle. Here, an Elder holds the talking piece and thanks the 8th and 3rd grade girls for the refreshments. Photo by Kaori Sakagami.

one another. Eye contact indicates that they respect each other, that they are open and honest, or that they are glad to see one another. Yet, in many other cultures, a younger person would not look an elder in the eye out of respect for the elder's wisdom and experience. A Muslim woman from Sierra Leone explained that her grandmother expects her to bow when she greets her. The grandmother has been to Mecca. She deserves the respect of a bow from her granddaughter for completing the pilgrimage.

Schools have rules, like no running in the halls, to ensure the safety of all students and staff. The expectation or rule to wear school uniforms may be intended to represent equality among all students, regardless of class or economic status. Games have rules to make sure that everyone plays fairly. There are rules or laws that require people who work with children and youth to report any suspected abuse of a child, because civil society values children and wants them to be safe and healthy. Oftentimes, schools make a new rule each time some confusion or trouble arises. But reviewing shared values can help to keep everyone going on a "good path" more effectively than imposing yet another rule.

A colleague of mine, Rick, told me how he solved the problem of a chronically absent student. The boy was ignoring the attendance rule, namely, that students must go to school unless they have a signed excuse from their parents. This student simply did not show up for days at a time. One day, Rick decided to illustrate what he explained on the first day of class: you are all important to our learning. So, he took his class outside the school and walked up the block to the absent student's house. They rang the doorbell. The student opened the door. Rick said, "We would like to have class with you, because we miss you and you are important. May we come in?" The boy let his classmates in. After that hour of home instruction, he was a regular participant in Rick's class in school.

Moving the dialogue up to the value—that everyone is important to our learning—was more effective for this student than going down to the rule. Making a new rule for him or imposing a punishment would not have been nearly as effective. So, participants first need to discuss their values before setting the common agreements or rules of a Circle.

One way to do this is to think, write, and speak in Circle. Give each student a small paper plate or piece of paper and colored markers. Ask them to think of what helps them learn and get along in the classroom and then write a word that expresses this on the paper plate. For example, they might come up with words like "respect," "fun," or "honesty." Then convene the Circle by introducing the talking piece. For an opening, explain the metaphor of the talking piece—what it represents to you or what it might mean for the class.

For introductions, ask the students to say their name and the word they wrote on the paper plate: "My name is Gus, and my word is 'truth,' because I believe we all have a part of the truth, and by sharing it, we can work together well."

As each word is introduced, the plate is added to the centerpiece on the floor. In the next few rounds, the group can explore the words with questions: "Is there a word that someone else put into the center that you would like to pick up and talk about, because you like that word a lot too?" "Is there a word you have a question about?" "Do any of these words contradict each other?"

After discussing the meaning of the words, the keeper may invite the students to illustrate one of the values with a story: "Pick one of the words on the plates, and share a story of when you felt the power of that word. For instance, I will take the word 'community.' I went to a picnic once where I knew no one, but the person who organized the picnic sat with me on my blanket. She explained some things about the school I was going to attend and shared her cookies with me. By the end of the picnic, I felt like I could be part of this school community. I felt welcomed." Finally, ask the students to talk about how they can contribute a value to the classroom: "People will know I respect them because I . . ."

The questions can move from the general to the personal to a challenge: "What do you value in this class?" "Share a time when you experienced that value." "The next time I see someone being left out, I will . . ."

A closing for this Circle about values can be as simple as a final pass with this question: "In one word, how was this Circle for you today?" Or, it can be specific: "Share a value you like other than the one you expressed today." It may help students who are new to the Circle for the keeper to encourage talking by taking the lead and answering each question first. Or, if everyone seems to understand, the keeper can pose the question and answer it herself at the end when the talking piece comes back around.

Jack Mangan, a behavior specialist in an inner-city K–8 school, closes his Circles by asking students to stand, touch each others' toes around the circle, and then give the talking piece to a student who is a leader-type and pose the question, "How did you think the Circle went today?" The toe-touching ending illustrates connectedness and gives students a safe, respectful way to touch. Asking a student to close the Circle would give that student the opportunity to lead in a good way.

At the end of the Circle, the paper plates can be gathered up and kept as part of the classroom. They can be posted, reviewed, used as spelling words, or used as prompts for writing projects. They can also tie in with other social skills curricula, such as character education, bullying prevention education, or social studies. Some people start their Circles by referring to values. In the introductory pass, each student can say his or her name and a value, even if they say no more than, "Sam, confidentiality." Quiet people are more likely to talk if you make it easy for them to put their voice into the room just once.

Guidelines

After the values of the Circle community have been discussed, then the common agreements or guidelines can be created. Here are some common questions that keepers use to start the discussion about agreements for the Circle:

- How do we need to act so that we are true to these values?
- What kind of guidelines for behavior do we need so that we follow these values?
- What do you need to feel safe in this classroom or in this Circle?

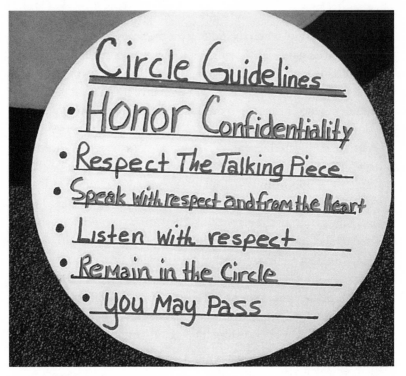

The St. Louis Park High School Circle guidelines were developed by the youth in the Circle. Photo courtesy of St. Louis Park High School (SLPHS).

Many keepers prefer to use the terms "common agreements" or "guidelines" rather than the word "rules." "Rules" suggest rigidity and are found in the student handbook, which is a legal document. Rules tend to be set by authorities. In Circles, the participants generate the guidelines, which everyone agrees to follow. The spirit of "guidelines" or "common agreements" can be found in the poetic agreement suggested by one boy in a middle school Circle: "Don't step on anyone else's dream."

Some basic agreements guide most Circles, and keepers can use these to help the class begin to develop its own list for a specific

Circle. The "You're the One Who Can Make the Peace" media campaign sponsored by the Minnesota Department of Public Safety published a flyer about using Circles in the classroom. It opened with some guidelines around the use of the talking piece:

When holding the talking piece, you show respect to the Circle and to each other by doing the following:

- speaking from the heart
- speaking with respect (no name-calling or put-downs)
- speaking briefly, so that everyone will have time to speak
- speaking on the topic.[3]

In her book of middle school Circle activities, *Behind the Green Glass Door*, written for the Minneapolis Public Schools, Marion London listed these common agreements:

- Everyone is respected.
- Everyone gets a chance to talk without interruption.
- We explain ourselves by telling our stories.
- Everyone is equal; no person is more important that anyone else.[4]

A youth group in a Minnesota high school uses the following guidelines. They are written on a piece of white tag board that can be carried easily to any room in which a Circle is conducted:

- Speak only when you have the "TP" (talking piece).
- Speak from your heart.
- Honor confidentiality.
- Listen with respect.
- No swearing.
- You may pass.

One of the most comprehensive resources for the Circle process is *Peacemaking Circles: From Crime to Community*.[5] In the book, authors Kay Pranis, Barry Stuart, and Mark Wedge describe the basic guidelines for Circles:

Along with additional guidelines participants may agree upon for a specific Circle, the following six guidelines are essential for Circle dialogues. Collectively, they translate the values and principles into concrete behavior that makes it easy for newcomers to adapt to the Circle atmosphere. These core guidelines are:

respect the talking piece;

speak from the heart;

speak with respect;

listen with respect;

remain in the Circle; and

honor confidentiality.[6]

Each Circle community develops its own guidelines. But, as these lists indicate, Circle groups tend to agree on the need for guidelines around the talking piece, listening and speaking with respect and from the heart, and confidentiality. One class developed their agreements by first listing on poster paper everyone's response to the question, "What would make the Circle a safe place for me?" Then they looked at all the suggestions and started grouping them into categories. Finally, they selected key words that all the students could agree on and made action statements around those words. These became their agreements. Instead of voting on the statements, they kept passing the talking piece around until everyone said, "Yes, I agree; I can live with these words." By taking the time to work things out in this way, the class was able to run their Circle smoothly for most of the year.

Ron and Roxanne Claassen state in their book *Discipline That*

Restores, "It is in making and keeping agreements that trust is built."⁷ The exercise of coming to consensus around guidelines gives students the chance to make simple agreements, follow them, and start to build trust with each other. Trusting that people will respect each other enhances the climate in the classroom, both socially and academically.

Occasionally, a class might decide that they want to review the agreements. For example, do they need to change the words, or do they simply need to follow them more closely? Usually, they find that the words work just fine, so they use the exercise to recommit to their agreements.

CHAPTER 5

Components of the Circle Process

The Keeper(s)

Jamie and Oscar came to the Circle training for teachers and school administrators with four students from a high school Circle that Oscar runs every week. Everyone sat in a circle, and Jamie started the session by reading a poem about awareness from a favorite poet. Then she introduced herself and the talking piece she brought—a long, hand-carved stick given to her by a mentor. She sent the stick around, asking each person to introduce himself or herself. When the talking piece came back to her, she invited Oscar and the students, who were sitting to her left, to talk about their Circle. As the stick made its way around the Circle, the participants asked the students questions, which they answered in the moment. Some people just offered comments, and some passed the stick without talking. When the stick got back to Jamie, she sent it around again for "anything else anyone had to say." People thanked the students or offered them praise for their insights. Being teachers, many suggested that the students go into education. Jamie took the stick and read a closing text from Martin Luther King Jr. The boys got up and ended the session, leading everyone in a handshake around the Circle.

The person who facilitates the Circle is called a "keeper," as I noted earlier. In *The Little Book of Circle Processes*, Kay Pranis describes the keeper as one who "assists the group in creating and maintaining a collective space in which each participant feels safe to speak honestly and openly."[1] According to *The Little Book of Restorative Discipline for Schools*, keepers "do not control the Circle, but help participants uphold its integrity."[2] They are equal participants in the Circle. "It is not a position of power, but it is a responsibility to others to keep to the values of the Circle."[3] Instead of running the process, the keeper *serves* it.

To be a teacher and a Circle keeper in the classroom present an interesting juxtaposition of roles. Generally, a teacher wants to be in control of his or her classroom—the ebb and flow, what is taught, what happens when. With Circles, however, it is the participants who ultimately set the flow. The keeper serves their interests and follows their lead. The teacher's goal in using Circles is the same as with any educational tool. The idea is that students eventually are able to use the knowledge or skill being taught for their own purposes. A Circle teacher not only lays the groundwork of skills but also encourages a sense of curiosity and wonder, so the students are inspired to take charge of their own learning. As Circle keeper, the teacher provides instruction and the opportunity to practice. Slowly, though, the keeper-teacher lets go of "what needs to be taught when" as the students become the keepers of their own Circles, as this story illustrates:

> *A breathless first-grader runs up to the school administrator supervising the playground. "Mrs. Ticiu, Mrs. Ticiu!" he exclaims, "I need a talking piece!" Mrs. Ticiu reaches into her pocket, extracts a small plastic dinosaur, and offers it to the child. He grasps the dinosaur tightly in his fist and dashes off to join several other students, who moments earlier, were arguing. With the help of the talking piece, they discuss their disagreement and find a solution they all like.*[4]

This may sound like utopia. However, just as we don't think twice when children start to read on their own, so, too, is it normal for students to use, on their own, well taught social skills.

Cindy Skalsky describes one approach she uses to teach the Circle process. She turns the Circle over to the students, posing the question of how they might improve both the school and themselves.

> What I did a couple of years ago with a challenging group of fifth graders was to introduce the Circle slowly. Then I would have one quick question for fun—"what do you think or feel about . . . ?" and "how can you solve it?" My question was, "If you could change one thing in this school, what would you change and why?" From that, several students indicated they didn't like the options for school lunches. So, I asked all of the class. We talked about what they thought or felt about school lunches, and then I asked, "What ideas do you have to improve it?" One student took notes and another typed up the ideas and shared it with the lunchroom staff. Some changes were made based upon their input.

Eventually, after we talked about their ideas to improve the school and other ideas about how to improve the world, we talked about what ideas they have on how we could improve this classroom or themselves. They ended up developing silent signals to remind each other not to gossip or talk behind each other's back. They developed a list of classroom rules that they felt were important, so students had a good environment to learn.[5]

How Does It Work? Ceremony and Storytelling

The process of speaking and listening in Circle is as simple as "circling up" some chairs, picking up a stress ball in the shape of an apple, and passing it to your left with a question that invites simple but thoughtful sharing: "Who are you?" "Why are you here today?" "What do you like?" "What problem do we need to solve together?" "How can we help?" A Circle keeper could then just follow her or his own intuition and the thoughts and interests of the group to complete a "Circle."

But Circle keepers and participants in and out of schools recognize core elements that organize the Circle process. These elements encourage a sense of safety, deep listening, and honest speaking. They also provide a framework for problem solving. Dimming or bringing up the lights signals the beginning of a concert or the intermission to a play. It sets the stage for listening and responding to a performance. So, too, there are ways of opening and closing a Circle and organizing the middle portion. Ceremony, ritual, and storytelling complete the space, while the wisdom and experience that Indigenous Peoples have with the talking Circle offers a deeper understanding of the process.

Some cultures open any social gathering with a prayer. It represents an intentional call to the participants to recognize the group, the purpose of the gathering, and the reality or presence of something that is greater than them. In the United States, common public openings include playing or singing the National Anthem or reciting the Pledge of Allegiance. People respond to these openings consciously, aware of the words and the symbolic meaning of the act. They can freely choose whether to participate or to respectfully watch. Opening rituals or ceremonies are intended to gather the group together and signal the beginning, whether the occasion is a meal, a wedding, a political debate, or a ball game.

Some American Indian people open a Circle with a prayer or with burning sage or sweetgrass, a process called "smudging." "Sage is a medicine in my life," said the late Chuck Robertson, Ojibwe and Dakota educator and Circle trainer. "Burning sage helps cleanse, clear, and open the mind." Besides its spiritual value, the opening signals the beginning of the process. It helps participants set aside other issues, so they can be present in the moment at the Circle. Likewise, the Circle may close with a prayer or good words that once again recognize the community, its work, and the beliefs and aspirations of the community to be together in a good way.

Children respond positively to rituals, namely, the intentional repetition of actions that signal something different and special. Think of the ritual of Thanksgiving dinner at your house or the ritual opening of a baseball game. Actors and athletes have rituals that they hope will prepare them mentally for performance or bring them luck. Establishing the routine or ritual of an ongoing Circle helps participants quickly focus on the current moment and be present to the process. In a public school or in any setting that includes multiple beliefs and cultures, the opening and closing of a Circle can provide symbolic welcome and, like the objects that are chosen for the centerpiece, suggest inclusion.

The most generic of openings is to invite students to sit in silence for a minute or to participate in simple yoga breathing. Regardless of where we come from—if we are tall or short, old or young—everyone has to breathe. Breathing together or inviting people to be intentional in recognizing their breathing calls attention to our similarities, despite our differences.

Oscar Reed, Circle keeper and trainer, tells of one of his first forays into using Circles with a group of special education, middle school students from the inner city: "I asked them to sit in silence for a minute—sixty seconds—and they would complain, 'Man, that is too long!' But once they got used to it, they could sit easily for two or three minutes. They always expected to be silent; sometimes they would ask for silence if I did not start the Circle that way." He concluded, "The kids seldom have silence in their world. They longed for it, once they discovered it."[6]

After people have taken time to be aware of their breathing and, hopefully, the present moment in which they sit, another part of opening the Circle can be added—a reading or story. The selection of the opening can further set the stage for the Circle. Stories illustrate values or problems. They provide perspective for the discussion that will follow.

Cordelia Anderson used the following story, one of the legends of the Cherokee People, to open a Circle with a group of middle school boys of different races who had continual scuffles on the playground.

The Wolves Within

An old Grandfather said to his grandson, who came to him with anger at a friend who had done him an injustice, "Let me tell you a story.

"I, too, at times have felt a great hate for those that have taken so much, with no sorrow for what they do.

"But hate wears you down, and does not hurt your enemy. It is like taking poison and wishing your enemy would die. I have struggled with these feelings many times." He continued, "It is as if there are two wolves inside me. One is good and does no harm. He lives in harmony with all around him and does not take offense when no offense was intended. He will fight only when it is right to do so, and in the right way.

"But the other wolf, ah! He is full of anger. The littlest thing will set him into a fit of temper. He fights everyone, all the time, for no reason. He cannot think because his anger and hate are so great. It is helpless anger, for his anger will change nothing.

"Sometimes, it is hard to live with these two wolves inside me, for both of them try to dominate my spirit."

The boy looked intently into his Grandfather's eyes and asked, "Which one wins, Grandfather?"

The Grandfather smiled and quietly said, "The one I feed."[7]

The story poses the question for the boys to answer: Which wolf would they feed? Would they work to build understanding and

COMPONENTS OF THE CIRCLE PROCESS ♦ 101

have control over their actions, or would they focus on fighting and anger? The story helped to frame the discussion that followed and quickened their insight. Thereafter, they could refer to "the wolves in their lives" as a metaphor for their personal challenges and their struggles to respond with insight. Anderson notes that this story provides a useful opening for a Circle on burnout with a school staff as well.

Chicken Soup for the Teenage Soul is a book I have seen used in many middle and high school Circles. *Bartlett's Familiar Quotations* or a quick search on the Internet can also help Circle keepers who are pressed for time to find pertinent openings. Literature, poetry, songs, and personal stories can provide the literal and the metaphorical direction for a Circle. One Circle keeper uses the metaphor or the symbolic meaning of a talking piece she has chosen for a Circle and the objects on the centerpiece to set the stage for a meaningful Circle.

Closing the Circle should also be obvious and predictable. Most Circles close with one final pass of the talking piece, so that everyone can essentially "check out." The Circle keeper may solicit final thoughts by asking, "In one word, how was this Circle for you?" or "Is there anything else anyone has to say?" Especially if the keeper is a teacher, he or she can use this last pass as another opportunity to look specifically and directly at each student, whether or not the student says something. Then the keeper closes the Circle. Closings can be formal with a reading of another quote or story, or they can be a summary of the discussion. A closing might also be a time for the keeper to highlight one idea discussed in the Circle. Or, the keeper can close with a simple, "Thank you for talking and listening today." A clear ending sends the signal to participants that it is time for them to transition from the Circle to their next activity: math, recess, lunch, or going home.

Once all the participants are present and the Circle has established its focus through the opening, the Circle becomes a space where people listen and speak. In *The Little Book of Circle*

Processes, Pranis outlines four elements of the Circle process. These elements first develop relationships and then focus them into action. They provide the general outline of the conversation:

1. Meeting, getting acquainted
2. Building understanding and trust
3. Addressing visions and issues (content)
4. Developing plans and a sense of unity.[8]

This outline is particularly helpful when participants are engaged in problem solving, such as a planning meeting or using a Circle to repair harm. Each element creates the foundation for the next. It is logical that people introduce themselves to each other, share their job or position, and make simple connections, which could be anything from agreeing on the weather to finding out if anyone has a mutual friend or common experience. Small talk helps people warm up before discussing whatever issues are at hand: from a staff meeting to sharing information to addressing a fight.

Getting Acquainted

After the opening (breathing, singing, listening to a reading, or silence), participants use the Circle space to meet and get acquainted. As the first pass, the keeper sends the talking piece around and invites participants to introduce themselves. "What is your name and what brings you to the Circle?" is one prompt for the beginning of a Circle. It also provides an easy way for students to "check in."

If the keeper invites people to say their name and answer a metaphorical question about how they are feeling, the answers can give the teacher and the other students insights into each student's emotional state that day. The questions could be direct. One alternative learning program asks the students at the

Wednesday weekly Circle to share a high and a low of the week so far. Or, the question could be less direct: What kind of weather are you today? If everyone feels partly cloudy or like a thunderstorm, perhaps a quiet session of journal writing could help them process what they are feeling and start the day with everyone being mindful of their emotions.

The routine of having students say their name as the first go-round helps them affirm their presence. As I mentioned before, getting students to speak just once can encourage verbal participation throughout the day. This opening round provides a simple way to do this: everyone can say his or her name. If a new person is in the Circle, he or she will hear each person's name and say his or her own. This is a naturally welcoming process and a quick way for a new student to learn names.

Building Understanding and Trust

Storytelling provides a natural way for people to connect, and it sets up a process for developing empathy. Students may see themselves in a peer's story of running to the bus on a snowy day and then falling down and getting all wet. Or, they might remember when they felt sad at the death of a pet, just like their classmate is feeling when she says her dog died. Collective narrative therapy practitioners David Denborough and Cheryl White point out that helping others tell their stories enables "people who are experiencing hardship to make a contribution to others who are also experiencing hard times. The experience of making a contribution sustains and generates hope."[9]

Social emotional learning practices and ideas can be applied in the "meeting, getting acquainted" phase of Circles. What students say in response to the quick opening question, for example, can give the Circle keeper ideas for the "building understanding and trust" element that follows. According to the Collaborative on Academic, Social and Emotional Learning (CASEL), "Social

and Emotional Learning (SEL) is the process of developing social and emotional skills in the context of a safe, caring, well-
managed, and engaging learning environment." SEL components
include self-awareness, responsible decision-making, relationships skills, social awareness, and self-management.[10]

All aspects of the Circle give students practice in developing
not just social skills but skills that are valuable for learning other
subjects as well. Certainly listening and speaking skills—essential
elements of communication—are enhanced through participating in Circles. Storytelling helps support literacy teaching. Students tell stories when they do journal writing or write fiction. By
hearing each other tell stories during Circles, they can begin to
hone their own skills for shaping a "beginning, middle, and end"
of a narrative. Including storytelling during a round of a Circle
can build students' confidence in their ability to stand up and
speak in front of peers when they go to speech class.

Circles are definitely a community-building process. The word
"building" suggests that the process is most effective when it is
used on an ongoing basis—regularly. It is not the best practice to
use a Circle only under certain circumstances or when trouble
arises. Building understanding and trust take time.

By building community, Circles serve preventive functions.
They strengthen relationships and increase protective skills and
assets. During regular Circles, misunderstandings are more
likely to surface and can be addressed constructively before
they erupt in conflicts or harmful behaviors. When harms do
occur, the stronger the relationships and the more skill and trust
students have in the Circle process, the more readily conflicts
can be resolved in a good way. Ongoing Circles create a positive
space that is already in place when difficult issues come up.

Using Circles to repair harm requires a deep understanding both of the Circle process and of how to apply restorative
principles. It also requires knowledge and skills about how
to conduct preparatory meetings or Circles before the main

Circle to address the harm. During these preparation gatherings, people—victims, offenders, and other affected parties—are invited to participate in a restorative process. These preparatory steps are well outlined in books on restorative measures, such as *Peacemaking Circles: From Crime to Community.* But skill in using the Circle process to repair harms also requires experiential training and Circle-keeping apprenticeships.

Used in classrooms, Circles typically have an opening and a closing. In the middle, they might include storytelling, sharing, reflecting on an assignment, or discussing a topic, depending on the situation. In any Circle, the process is deliberate, thoughtful, and intentional.

Confidentiality

I was once called to a parents' meeting at a small charter school. The school had recently started using the Circle process as a way to hold their daily class meetings. This practice had become controversial for some parents. At the meeting, it did not take long to find out that they were concerned with what one parent called the "secrecy of Circle." It seems that children had come home and with enthusiasm said, "We have this really great way to talk in school. It is called a Circle." "Really," the parents replied, "and what do you talk about?" "Oh, I can't tell you," the children would say. "It's a secret."

The elementary-age children had taken very seriously a common guideline for Circles, namely, "What is said in Circle stays in Circle." They did not yet have the skills to explain the process and to give a summary of what happens in a typical Circle meeting. The idea of secrets in a classroom would raise interest, if not concern, with any engaged parent.

Once the purpose of the confidentiality guideline was explained, however, parents were more inclined to give the new process a chance. When they learned that they were invited to participate in any classroom Circle at any time, the tension in the room subsided considerably.

"What is said in Circle stays in Circle" is a commonly agreed-upon Circle guideline. Yet Circle members may agree together on what may be shared outside of the Circle. Keeping the confidentiality of Circle communication encourages honest conversation. Participants are more ready to share deeply held values, beliefs, and feelings. If the other members of the Circle can truly honor this sharing, then the guideline can help students develop empathy, caring, and connection among all involved. Deeper, more serious conversations can be held—conversations that can enhance feelings of safety and respect even in trying times.

For instance, a group of multi-cultural, multi-political high school students gathered once a week for a one-credit semester course in Circle after the September 11 (2001) attacks in New York and Washington, DC, and during the first months of the war in Afghanistan. Feelings ran high regarding what was happening in the world: the attacks, patriotism, racism, classism, religion, war in general, and a war in Afghanistan in particular. The students were glad for a place to talk, and the agreement, "What is said in Circle stays in Circle"—confidentiality—enhanced the process. "I was able to respect someone who was so opposite of what I believed, because of our talk in Circle," one young woman said later. "I had to listen, and even though I did not agree—would never agree—I found a way to see him as an honest person with honestly held ideas. It was hard. Keeping confidentiality made the discussion safe."

This seventeen-year-old high school student had the skills to convey the flavor and feeling of the Circles she participated in without breaking the confidentiality of her fellow students. The second graders had not yet developed these communication skills. Part of teaching the Circle process to students and adults is to help them understand how to tell the "story" of the Circle.

I recommend starting with helping students understand what is personal in nature. For example, the names of the persons who told stories about their experiences or feelings should be kept in Circle. However, general topics, such as "we talked about families," "we talked about pets and hobbies," or "we had an intense talk about the election" are okay to describe to others outside the Circle.

Another teacher offered her students this guidance: "Speak about what you said, not about what others said, unless you have their permission to do so." Yet in some situations, telling the story of the Circle is precisely what everyone in the Circle wants. For instance, students from an English Language Learners program and students from an Alternative Learning Center told the following story at a state conference as part of a workshop on the use of Circles to repair harm.

A group of newly arrived Karen students from Myanmar (Burma) got into a fight on a bus with a group of American students. Both groups attended the same small school but were in different programs. Neither group spoke the other's language. This inability to communicate was part of the reason for the fight. Students agreed to sit in Circle with a translator, the school principal, two educational aides (one African American, the other Karen), and the Circle keeper, who was the school's social worker.

Doing a Circle with a translator provided a lot of insight for everyone participating. The process slowed way down, as the translator had to repeat everything anyone said. It showed how complicated communication can be and how much time it takes for people to learn about each other. The participants agreed to go back to their friends and tell them about the Circle, explaining that everyone in the Circle had agreed not to fight. In this situation, transparency and openness were essential to the success of the Circle process.

In other instances, however, honoring the confidentiality guideline—"what is said in Circle stays in Circle"—is essential.

Learning how to tell the story of the Circle, as in a Circle to teach elementary school students social skills, is important. Telling others the story of a Circle that was convened to repair harm can show that there was accountability and agreement. This knowledge can help a community to heal, as the bus-fight incident illustrates.

The confidentiality guideline is not about secrecy but about learning respect, discretion, and how to develop trust, so that people feel safe enough to share openly. Even in the simplest, most topic-focused Circles, deeper sharing can surface unexpectedly when confidentiality is ensured. To ensure that all involved have the same expectation of confidentiality for a particular Circle, Circle keepers can ask, "What will we tell others about this Circle?" Coming together with the mutual intent to share and to care for the feelings of the other participants allows people to express their feelings honestly. Participants can assume a baseline of respect and trust, assured that their emotional vulnerability will not be used against them.

Hopefully, two things will prevail: common sense and a respect for the Circle community. Circles help students of any age learn how to respect each other by not using personal information about others in mean ways. The fact that a girl is sad because her cat died or a boy is worried about his uncle in the military does not become a focus for teasing or taunting. Developing respect is part of the skill building that Circles offer. If the keeper or any member of the Circle is concerned about how personal information shared in Circle might be used, then this concern should become part of the Circle discussion. This very discussion can help foster deeper respect among the participants.

Handling Disclosures

Children may tell adults whom they trust any number of things. Sometimes, what they say may be that someone is harming them, that they may be harming themselves, or that they are harming someone else. If you are a teacher, this could come up in math class or in Circle. However, it is less likely that a disclosure of harm will occur in a math Circle on integers than in a Circle to repair harm.

Adults who work with children—teachers and other school personnel included—are required to contact Child Protection if they suspect that a child is being neglected or physically or sexually abused by a family member. All fifty states have passed some form of a mandated reporting law. Professionals must report suspected child abuse or neglect in order for their school, agency, program, or institution "to qualify for funding under the Child Abuse Prevention and Treatment Act."[11]

Telling students about mandated reporting in language that they can understand is important for Circles to repair harm. Circle participants may share personal concerns if they feel that they will be respected in Circle. Students may see a teacher, a student-support staff member, or a coach as a trusted adult, because they see the adult treating them with respect and listening closely to them in Circle.

Safe Place

As students and teachers discuss values, share objects and describe their meaning, make meaning out of ribbon and sticks, and decide together how best to run their Circle, a sense of safety may begin to develop. Students and staff take risks in speaking, because they believe they will be heard and respected. Increasing students' sense of safety can aid them academically. They will be better able to concentrate on lectures, studies, and reading without added emotional stress. They will also be more able to work together on projects without fear of being teased or bullied, put down, or excluded. Likewise, if students feel safe, they will be more likely to ask questions during class, which gives teachers cues as to what students understand and what they need more help in mastering.

Using Circles regularly in a classroom helps to develop a sense of safety. An art exercise can even focus on the issue of safety specifically, providing food for thought and discussion about the concepts of safety, academic safety, and the phrase "safe place."

For instance, provide each student a blank piece of paper and markers, crayons, or pencils. Ask students to draw a picture of a place where the physical environment helps them feel good, comfortable, welcome, or secure. For some, it may be their house or a place where their family goes on vacation. It may be an imaginary location, or it may be the neighborhood basketball court. I find the backstage of a theater during a performance a very safe place—warm, welcoming, comfortable, and exciting all at once.

After the students have drawn their picture, discuss the pictures in Circle. As with the values plates, each drawing can be placed on the floor around the circle and later, if the students agree, displayed on the classroom wall.

Passing

People will talk openly when they feel safe, and one way to cultivate that feeling is for participants to have a choice about what they say or do. In Circle, each person has a choice about whether to speak, to pass, or to hold the talking piece in silence for a time. The choice to pass in Circle is to be honored. Teachers sometimes feel uneasy if a student does not speak. But some children are introverts who simply may not want to speak in a group one day, or they take their time processing. They may well have something brilliant to say at the next Circle. Be warmly encouraging about speaking, but also allow the option to pass. Allowing participants to pass indicates that you respect their privacy. Showing such respect will lay the groundwork for future Circles. Allowing someone to pass may actually encourage speaking.

Circle keeper Jamie Williams encourages people to "have patience for silence," as it can be a powerful tool. She continues,

"When no one speaks, I 'use' the silence to speak for itself. Silence isn't just the absence of sounds; it is a living quality and promotes community when explored."

Ali Anfinson, a Circle keeper and trainer, speaks of the "rule of three" for passing around the talking piece. "Passing the talking piece around three times on a topic or questions usually elicits a response or comment from everyone in the Circle. For some people, they need time to process the question and process what others say before they wade into the discussion." Patience on the part of the keeper and other Circle members may be richly rewarded.

Kay Pranis tells of one Circle and the shift that transpired with each pass of the talking piece. Sitting in a Circle with a fifteen-year-old boy and his mother, one man passed (chose not to speak) the first time the talking piece went around, but on the second pass, he spoke up. "At first I was thinking, how could you do such stupid things that cause so much trouble for your mother? I was thinking like a parent. But now I am remembering what I was like as a teen. I think I understand better what you are dealing with." This remark changed the tenor and focus of the Circle conversation for everyone; the next round addressed the man's insight and allowed the boy to explore his behavior more critically.

Trainer and Circle keeper Terry Anfinson noted that, in sentencing Circles, people need three times around to start generating ideas for an agreement that are centered on relationships.

At first, Circle members would suggest fines or even jail time. On the second pass, the conversation would be about getting all As in every subject. But on the third pass, people would come up with practical, doable ideas for repairing the harm, such as, "Can you shovel the walk and driveway of the person you harmed?" "Can you commit to doing the dishes every night for your parents?" "How about helping the teacher with research on the next unit?" The third time around, people would think about relationships and about how people could give back to the community in a real way.[12]

In teaching the Circle process, particularly to younger children, some keepers have found it beneficial to cover other aspects of the Circle process before introducing the idea of passing. Cindy Skalsky describes the way she teaches students the Circle process:

When I introduce talking Circles, I introduce only one rule at a time. Only the person holding the talking piece has a right to speak. I use questions that are fun and simple that anyone can answer. I learned the hard way not to introduce the right to pass right away. Kids get hooked on sharing. Then when we need to get to feelings and opinions, the right to pass will be introduced. Teachers who have introduced it this way have had little to no problems with students thinking it is cute to pass and mocking those who say anything.[13]

Circle in the Square

The shape of a circle has no beginning or end, making it an ideal, practical arrangement for talking or meeting with others. Think of its earliest use, when a family or clan sat around the fire at night. Sitting in rows on a winter night in front of a fire would have been impractical and dangerous—the folks in back would have been pretty cold, if not frozen, by dawn.

The architecture of the Circle provides natural controls. Think of an ordinary classroom. The desks are in rows or clusters. The teacher and the students cannot see everyone at the same time. It seems to be just ordinary human nature that students think that they can have side conversations in the back corner of the room. After all, they are so far away from the teacher, and the other students cannot see them unless they have eyes in the back of their heads. Who is to know or, for that matter, care?

And side talking is not limited to students. I have presented to many a staff meeting and observed similar behaviors among the adults. I have done it myself. It seems so easy. The speaker is so far away, and who is being bothered? Desks and a table contribute not only to side conversations but also to side texting and side checking of smart phones for messages.

In Circle, however, everyone can see everyone else. The teacher or keeper does not need to spend too much energy policing side conversations. The people who are looking at cell phones are obvious. Everyone can see who is talking, just as everyone can see who has the talking piece. The shape of the Circle provides a natural control that encourages respectful behavior.

How, then, can one have a Circle when the desks are screwed to the floor, or when the district budget is so small that the class size has ballooned to thirty-five students in a room designed for twenty-four? The talking piece offers some small help in these situations. However, the keeper has to do more to ensure that the piece is honored—that is, that whoever holds the talking piece is given the chance either to speak or to hold it in silence. One teacher in a middle school used a three-foot-long peacock feather as the class talking piece: pretty charming and easily seen, in spite of rows.[14]

Another teacher holds fifteen-minute Circles with the students as they stand circling the classroom. While not ideal for a long Circle, standing serves numerous functions—providing students with a break from sitting, some movement, and, of course, practice in patience. Standing in place for fifteen minutes is good training for waiting to vote in a highly contested election, buying tickets for a playoff game, waiting for the bus or subway, or standing in line to get on the newest ride at the amusement park.

Consensus

Fires and feathers aside, the Circle is a basic communication process. Like Robert's Rules of Order, it ensures that people can communicate, deliberate, and make decisions in a good and fair way. Robert's Rules of Order depend upon the facilitator's skill and on all the participants knowing the rules in order for communication to proceed and for the decision-making to be fair. Participants can be at a distinct disadvantage if they do not know how to "Call the questions" or if they do not know that a "second" is needed to put forth a motion. In Robert's Rules of Order, decisions are made through votes and majority rule. Unless a decision is unanimous, this means that someone is always in the minority; there is always someone who has to accept the loss. The process offers participants ample opportunities to practice humility.

The Circle process also offers a way of communicating, deliberating, and making decisions. Instead of using a facilitator to call on people who would like to speak, however, the facilitator of a Circle—the keeper—passes the talking piece around the circle, which gives all the participants a chance to speak. Decisions are made not by voting and majority rule but through consensus. This process takes longer. People need time to deliberate. They have to explore possible solutions or decisions that incorporate all the viewpoints and ideas that have been raised. The goal is to devise an agreement that everyone can support.

Even though coming to consensus may be slower than voting to make a decision, the benefits are enormous and can even save time in the long run. With majority rule, there are clear winters and losers. The losing minority may well feel that they are then free to try to get what they want in other ways. They may seek legal action, like challenging a decision in court, or they may pursue non-legal means to change the ultimate outcome. In a school, this may take many forms—anything from subtly undermining a decision through gossip and misrepresentation, to not fulfilling terms of an agreement, to refusing to act on the agreement at all, to insubordination. In the most serious situations, the minority may seek retaliation against the majority.

If all the people affected by some harm—say, a fight—come together in Circle, then they as a group must reach consensus on how to repair the harm, how to make amends, how to help all those who have been hurt, and how to give back to the community. The likelihood of all these things actually happening, then, is much greater than if a principal simply told the students who were fighting to "leave each other alone." Active participation and having a true voice in decisions is the glue that can hold people together through an agreement. The inclusive, respectful, and authentic nature of the process helps people actually do what they said they would do. And if they do not follow through, then they simply have to get back in Circle and work it out.

A Somali story tells of a man who had several sons. As they grew, they began to fight with each other. The father was in danger of losing his farm because his sons were so busy fighting that they were not attending to the animals and the crops. So, he called them all together and gave each of them a stick. He asked them to break the stick. Being strong young men, they could do so easily. Then he gathered all the broken sticks into a bundle, tied it, and gave it to the sons. He said, "Now break the sticks." They could not. "You must work together," he said, "or your enemies will easily break you, one by one, like a single stick."

Likewise, the consensus process makes a bundle of sticks and ties it together through the process of everyone accepting the agreement in front of everyone else. Retaliation is less likely, because everyone agrees publicly. This agreement is not forced or imposed. It is authentic. Everyone has spoken from their hearts about their issues, needs, and concerns, and the group has listened. The consensus agreement takes into consideration what everyone has expressed, so that everyone can agree to it. The agreement embodies the combined wisdom and experiences of all the participants together. This is why it takes time.

The time spent working toward an agreement pays off. Completing the actions in an agreement is more likely, because the "sticks are standing" with each other. The student is not out in the community alone but is supported by all the people who came to consensus with him or her. Surveys indicate that Circle agreements and restorative conferencing agreements are completed 95–100 percent of the time.[15] These high rates of completion and follow-through hold because the communication process is clear and because everyone takes part in forming the agreement and accepts it. Because decisions are made by consensus, agreements carry the strength of the community to hold people to their word. Everyone becomes part of the strong bundle of sticks.

When given responsibility, students are true to their word. They have high expectations of each other. When I trained students to perform in *Touch*, the child sexual abuse prevention play I mentioned earlier, I witnessed the capacity youths have for building mutual trust. As actors, we talked about the importance of being able to trust each other on stage, so that we could perform a play on a difficult and sensitive subject. Trust meant that mistakes made in rehearsal or in performance stayed within the company. The last thing any actor needs is for the school to know how she muffed a line or how he dropped the prop and blew the scene. The student actors always took this seriously, and if anyone did talk out of turn, the cast called them on it. As I learned at the elementary school parent meeting, the high expectation of confidentiality—"what is said in Circle stays in Circle"—can be met even by first graders.

Free Expression of Feelings

The Circle process allows participants to express their feelings freely, as long as they are respectful in how they do this. Yet, some adults are uncomfortable with students expressing feelings during a Circle. Sometimes they say, "I am not a social worker" or "I don't want to do any touchy-feely things; I teach." It is as if feelings are the domain of people who have certain degrees, instead of something that all human beings experience. Children learn about feelings and how they are expressed just by being around adults—in school, in the grocery store, at home, on the playground, and in the media. Teachers teach their subject, and they teach how to be a human being.

Sometimes the answer to the question, "How are you?" is, "I am sad" or "I'm afraid." The human condition is such that people have accidents, they get sick, and people they know die. Even during simple check-ins, it is entirely possible that a person might cry in Circle. Something about feeling safe allows feelings to flow.

But Circle is not therapy. Neither the keeper nor any other Circle participant has to heal or fix a person's tears or anger. It is a place, though, where sympathy can be expressed, where people can see the sadness or hear anger, be present for it, and offer care. Listening is offering care. Listening is an action. Children can learn from our response.

If a child expresses grief or shares an experience of a traumatic event, the teacher can offer to the child an opportunity outside of Circle to meet with someone from the student support staff, such as a social worker, counselor, school nurse, or even the principal. So, if someone cries in Circle, everyone can learn to listen with care. They can say, "I am sorry you are sad," "I am sorry this happened to you," and ask, "Would you like to talk about this more?" This is a life skill, one that can be used over and over again.

While the criminal justice system in Minnesota started exploring the use of Circle sentencing in the mid-1990s based on a model from the Tlingit First Nation in Yukon, Canada, teachers had been using talking sticks and Circles in classrooms well before that. For instance, the Friends School of Minnesota developed the *I-to-I Conflict Resolution Curriculum* in 1988. It uses "two basic techniques: conferences or I-to-I's, and group gatherings or sharing Circles."[16] With the curriculum, teachers use the Circle process as a means of conducting group problem-solving sessions as well as class meetings.

Even before the Friends School curriculum, elementary school teachers in Minneapolis public schools used the "Magic Circle" to start or end the day. Magic Circle was a self-esteem and drug abuse prevention program used in the district elementary classrooms in the early 1980s. Marion London served as a teacher and trainer in the district. "The teachers and students sat in a circle, and, even though there was no talking piece, communication went around in order. Everyone had a chance to share. There was no judgment and no grade. It was all about kids having a say in their education. I thought, 'This is a cool thing!'"

London developed a number of prevention education curricula, including Project Charlie and Peaceful Partners: "With Project Charlie, the content was delivered while the kids were at their desks, but then I would have them do an activity in a circle.

"We would use a feeling cube in the circle," she said. "The kids liked it, and so I started all activities with the cube. It became our talking piece. When I learned about restorative measures and the Circle process from that vantage point, it resonated with all my other experiences, with the feeling cube, the morning meeting from Responsive Classroom, Olweus's class circle, the old Magic Circle. I heard this here and that there, but the RJ Circle put it together." Giving voice to students, she noted, strengthens their sense of connection. "It is good education," she said.[17]

Spirituality

Mel welcomed everyone to the Circle. He invited people to sit for a bit in silence and let our travel to the workshop for the day leave our minds. He offered a prayer in the Ojibwe

language for everyone and for the earth. He translated the
prayer. He held up the eagle feather and explained its sig-
nificance: the eagle is the link between the earth and the
creator, a messenger.

Then the feather went around for people to introduce
themselves—name, agency or school, and why they came to
the session on historical trauma. Mel told a story about his
father's experiences with several Indian boarding schools.
The feather went around. Participants shared many things:
their knowledge, their sadness for the pain of history, their
guilt for not knowing more, experiences with families, new
insights they now had about students they worked with,
concerns about relatives, as well as technical information
about working with children who have been hurt.

Another round brought out resources, ideas for inter-
ventions, and policy changes. Some people committed to
actions—pursuing further research, getting more training,
talking to a colleague, and changing a practice.

The final round was short. Mostly, people thanked
Mel and each other for insight, honesty, and for listening.
Mel ended the Circle with a saying from his grandmother
about joy.

The Circle embraces and reflects many of the spiritual values of
Indigenous Peoples in North America—values such as respect,
honor, compassion, forgiveness, and generosity. But we need to
distinguish between the Circle as a communication process,
teaching process, or problem-solving process and spiritual practices. "The Circle in itself is not a ceremonial practice of Indigenous people," explained Stephanie Autumn, member of the Hopi
Nation and a restorative justice practitioner. "In Indigenous
communities, the Circle is utilized by Indigenous people to repair harm, strengthen relationships, and improve communication, to find learning-based outcomes and equitable solutions."[18]

I have heard two main concerns raised in school settings by non-Indigenous adults about using Circles. One concern is that, by using the Circle process, a religious practice is being expropriated by the majority culture and used in ways far from its original meaning and intent. Other people see the Circle process as "an American Indian ceremony" and, as such, they believe it doesn't belong in a public school.

"In my experience," Autumn said, "there has been a common misunderstanding of the Circle process and values being an Indigenous ceremony by many non-Indigenous people. Some Indigenous Circle facilitators bring 'cultural items' for use as the talking piece or to place in the center of the circle. While those items can be identified as 'sacred' to Indigenous people and used in Indigenous ceremonies, the Circle process is not a traditional ritual or ceremony."[19]

Not surprisingly, Circle keepers who are American Indian follow their own set of practices. An American Indian teacher working in an American Indian magnet school, for instance, may use one kind of talking piece in part to teach the cultural meaning of the object. Others may introduce themselves in their Native language but would not begin with a prayer. Laurie Vilas, a trainer, Circle keeper, and member of the White Earth Band of Ojibwe, talked about conducting a Circle to repair the harm of vandalism. Because all of the participants in the Circle were members of her Nation, she assumed that all would appreciate an opening prayer in Ojibwe. However, some of the participants were Christian and objected. "I learned never to make assumptions," she said. "Now I ask people what would be a good way to open the Circle."

I first learned about Circle use in the classroom when I read about a teacher using a talking stick to teach students about an African tribe's cultural practices. Besides learning about American Indian, especially Ojibwe, Circle practices, I have also learned a bit about the Xeer Soor or traditional Somali restorative justice process. In the Somali countryside, the elders would sit in a circle under a tree and handle village disputes, marital conflicts, or crime. People had to repair harm in order to keep the peace.

Child development theory describes the importance of looking at the whole child and of attending to the emotional, physical, mental, and social development of each child. Similarly, the Medicine Wheel epitomizes the philosophy of many Indigenous Peoples. It provides the philosophy and values underlying Circles, which encourages a "whole" worldview. The Medicine Wheel is divided into four quadrants that can represent many things, among them the physical, emotional, mental, and spiritual aspects of life. In *Peacemaking Circles: From Crime to Community*, Pranis, Stuart, and Wedge discuss the way in which the Medicine Wheel philosophy describes being human:

We're not only matter or only mind, neither are we only our emotions or even only spiritual beings. We are all these together—physical, mental, emotional, and spiritual. All four facets are essential to our existence, and they must be balanced for an activity to be successful or for a person, family, or community to be healthy.[20]

In community practice, Circles can start with prayer, good words, a quote, or a song, as long as all the participants agree and would feel welcomed by such an opening. In a public school, however, building a Circle community must start with the recognition that the students are diverse: religiously, socioeconomically, ethnically, and otherwise. Each group, which most likely includes this diversity, establishes its own ways of opening a Circle.

Around one hundred different languages are spoken in Minnesota public schools—urban, suburban, rural, and tribal.

Minnesota is more than Lake Wobegon. It is a tapestry of the original keepers of the land—the Dakota, Ho-Chunk, and Ojibwe Nations—as well as all who immigrated here, were forced here, and all who continue to come here.

Yet within this diversity are shared values. Children have a common need to see that they are part of a larger whole. Oral stories, literature, and poetry provide us with a way both to articulate common values and to illustrate differences. A moment of silence at the beginning of a Circle offers each student and staff person the chance to at least breathe and be aware of where he or she is at that moment in time. We know oxygen is required for brain function.

The opening routine at one school Circle is to circle up, sit in silence for a minute, and read a quote from one of the historical figures whom the class is studying. Then they go around, say their name, and mention one common agreement that they appreciate that day (the agreements have been posted on the wall). To start the discussion, they each respond to a check-in question, such as "How was the weekend?' "If you were a bird today, what kind of bird would you be?" "What is your favorite dessert?" "What did you think about the hockey game last night?"

Taking time to be present, to connect to each other, to discuss a value shared by the group, and to sit in silence—this can be sacred for any participant. It can also be comforting for any participant, or it can be routine. People bring who they are to the Circle and take what they need. Mostly, the process needs to be conducted in a way that is comfortable for everyone and can evolve as the community grows in appreciation of each other.

Our stories are our lives. Even if a story is made up or has only half-truths in it, the story tells the listener something about who the teller is as a person. When we tell a story, we are exposed. It is an act of humanity, and it connects us to our selves, to each other, and to our ancestors. Telling our stories can be a spiritual act, wherever and whenever it is shared.

A group of teachers and administrators had been participating in a Circle training for two days. They had engaged in an exercise where they role played—with great accuracy—middle school students. The laughter subsided, and the talking piece—a spiral bookmark made of recycled aluminum—went around to discuss the role-play. The conversation turned to important teachers they had had in their lives: the coach who expected high grades and high jumps; the math teacher who gave them a second chance; and the janitor who asked, "Do you know who your dad was?"

Janice then told the story: "My dad died when I was six. He was a principal, but I never really knew him. When I was in eighth grade, I started running with a fast crowd, and we started skipping school and such. One day, the janitor pulled me out from a group of kids who I think were getting ready to fight. He said, 'I've been watching you. This is not your path. This is not you.' He took me to his office and gave me a carved wooden apple. I kid you not. He said it was given to him by my dad. I did not know this man, but he knew my dad, because he was a student in Dad's school. He said when he was in middle school, he was going the same way I was. He had gotten arrested even. But my dad talked to him, followed him, watched him, asked him for his homework even before his teachers did. Because of my dad, this man graduated, got a job, and now has a family. Not everyone in his family had the same outcome. I took that apple, and I still have it. On my desk. Next to my framed PhD. Next to the pictures of my family. I never really knew my dad, but that man, he let me know who my dad was, and who I am.

CHAPTER 6

Teacher Testimony

Everyone files into the classroom and takes his or her place. The
desks are set in a circle—kind of tight because the room was made
for a smaller class. A copy of the U.S. Constitution is the talking
piece. As it goes around the circle, students in the history class
check in as their favorite historical character—LaShawn as Dred
Scott; Markus as George Washington; Lisa as Eleanor Roosevelt.
The teacher takes Thurgood Marshall. Then he outlines the sched-
ule of the period and begins the lesson.

Using the Circle process to repair harm requires training and
practice, a strong grounding in the theory of restorative justice,
and knowledge about the dynamics of victims, offenders, and
bystanders. But the Circle process itself—a process for ensuring
that all people are able to speak and actively participate, whether
as speaker or as listener—is pretty straightforward. Teachers
and youth workers have adapted the process to the classroom
in a variety of ways. Here are two descriptions of how the Circle
process is being used in the classroom to deliver content and to
engage students in learning.

Angela Wilcox writes about her work as a language arts
teacher. She first learned about Circles when the staff at the urban
recovery school where she worked participated in a three-day
Circle training in 2002. (Different from a traditional high school,
a "recovery school" is an alternative learning center where the
students have all been in treatment for chemical dependency

and are seeking a learning environment that supports their sobriety.)[1] The school started using Circles for students to "check in" at the beginning of the week and to "check out" at the end of the week. The school also began using Circles to repair harm. Angela then took the process into her classroom as the creative writing teacher at PEASE (Peers Enjoying A Sober Education) Academy and later into her current position as a language arts and social studies middle school teacher in Hopkins, Minnesota.

Teaching Writing in Circle

by Angela Wilcox

It was mid-August when I walked into my new English classroom at the alternative school where I had recently accepted a teaching position. I was excited and wary as I considered the challenges of teaching every student in grades 8–12 in the same classroom. What I hadn't expected was the response I'd receive to my question about where the classroom materials were stored. Where were the books? Textbooks? Was there anything that had been used in the past few years to teach language arts? They didn't exist, I was told. It seems that the previous teacher had facilitated a "conversation hour" and given students credit for speech. This fulfilled their English credits for high school graduation.

And so was launched a fascinating chapter in my teaching career. I quickly realized that my students' lives contained stories enough to replace any textbook written. The teaching challenge was that these stories were unformed, oral, and unlikely to appear on paper without significant coercion. These students were not motivated by grades, credits, or their teacher's fine opinion of their hard work. Yet, they were showing up, and I was determined to make something happen.

Inspired by Nancie Atwell's reading and writing workshops, I formed a curriculum in which students chose their own books to read from an ever-evolving treasure trove of books I gathered from used book sales and donations from everyone I'd ever met.[2] I gave students time in class to read and to do their own writing. Following Atwell's suggestions for inspiring student writing as well as her "mini-lesson" format for introducing the key ideas students need to master in a language arts class, I was relieved when we got off to a bumpy but happy start. Students were writing their stories with varying levels of skill, and I was partway to my goal of bringing students' voices and stories into the curriculum.

I tried holding voluntary "read-aloud" days. Students could present a piece of writing they were developing to the class. Two or three students loved this and volunteered to read anything they could jot down on paper, sometimes to their classmates' chagrin. The quality of the writing was, at best, variable. The pool of volunteers never grew beyond that small group, despite offers of extra credit. My attempt to make the read-aloud mandatory was met by silent gazes. I then tried to create a communal reading of student work. I made copies of each student's favorite piece of writing and distributed them to the class. The students were to read each piece of writing, make comments, and return the piece to its author. At the end of the class period, though, I would find papers scattered under tables with scrawled queries of "wanna go to McDonalds for lunch??" across three-line poems. Clearly, the students did not see this as "real" writing. If they produced anything at all, it was to placate me, the teacher.

I realized that I had to find some way to invest the writing process with a sense of meaning and to build a sense of community in the classroom that would help students trust both themselves and each other. For several years, I tried a variety of techniques, writing styles, point systems, and exercises with varying degrees of success, but the classroom never came together as a community of writers as I hoped and imagined.

Then, a confluence of events brought me the keys I had been seeking. First, I found a book by Linda Christensen called

Reading, Writing and Rising Up.[3] In it, she talks about creating a community of writers in her classroom by staging something she calls the "read-around." All students are expected to participate, and each student both presents a piece of writing and gives feedback to the other writers in the circle. She speaks of the power of the read-around to engage students who otherwise feel disenfranchised by traditional teaching methods. She also describes the effectiveness of a read-around in a classroom where students' skills and needs vary widely. Her description struck me as the ultimate student-centered classroom, which was exactly what I was striving to create.

At the same time, our school was chosen as a pilot site for training in restorative justice philosophies and practices. The entire staff was able to participate in three days of training, which included extensive practice in Circle processes. We were all buzzing with the possibilities of building Circles into our school community, and it occurred to me that using a Circle and a talking piece might be the key to overcoming some of the challenges I'd encountered in trying to get students to share their writing. Because Circles are predicated on trust and center on the act of listening, I hoped they would provide the sense of safety and legitimacy that had been missing in the other methods, which were clearly not doing the trick.

The final important piece emerged from a writing class I was taking at The Loft Literary Center in Minneapolis. My teacher emphasized the importance of feedback and stressed that we had to be selective about what kind of feedback we solicited and from whom. I knew from my own experiences as a writer that one careless comment from the wrong person could destroy both my confidence and my interest in a piece of writing. By contrast, the right kind of feedback could inspire me to rework a piece a dozen times.

Our teacher gave us an article by Rosanne Bane, and this article helped me provide students with a concrete tool. Bane's seven levels of feedback empower writers to define exactly what kind of commentary and analysis would be helpful to them with a piece of writing. The framework allows students to consider their level of trust in the group, their confidence in a particular piece of writing, and the stage in the writing process before inviting others to comment.[4]

When writers present a piece of writing with heavy emotional content, for example, they may not be ready to hear feedback about the punctuation mistakes right away. Bane's tool allows them to define for themselves what they need from others. With these new ideas buzzing in my head, I started out the school year determined to bring student writing into the center of my curriculum.

With my own confidence in using the Circle process still evolving, I chose to wait to see how Circles worked in the school community at large before bringing them into my classroom. At the start of the new school year, we implemented a daily "check in" Circle. The talking piece was passed, and participants (staff and students) shared their names and a high and low point of their day. It was a simple way to build a sense of community. More than that, it was a beautiful way to introduce the concept of Circles to our students and to reinforce it on a daily basis. We could establish Circle norms and get people used to the talking piece in a nonthreatening and enjoyable way.

Once the concept of Circle was established, we were able to introduce Circles for reflection and discussion. Eventually, we began using Circles to confront difficult issues in our community. Students quickly developed a level of familiarity and comfort with Circles that did not require us to "train" them in a formal way. After two or three weeks had passed, I felt ready to introduce writing Circles into my language arts curriculum.

I started by giving students models of poetry and simple poetic forms that they could play with. Acrostics, sentence stems, and other low-risk forms lent themselves to the variety of students and skill levels in my classroom. I gave them writing workshop time in class, and I made rhyming dictionaries, thesauruses, correction fluid, and other writers' tools available.

I did a formal check-in with each writer at the start of the workshop time, asking them to tell me what they were working on and how they were progressing with their piece of writing. They watched me log this information on my clipboard. This sent a clear message that they were doing serious work, and that I was holding them accountable by giving them points for using their time well. I was available to conference with students about their writing, offer suggestions and resources, and push them to keep pushing themselves.

After students had had sufficient workshop time to create several pieces of writing, I asked them to read through their work and choose a piece of writing that they wanted some feedback on. I told them that the piece they selected may not be their "best" but could be the piece they were struggling with most. I then made copies of each piece they chose, so that the writers in the Circle could each have a copy.

I then introduced Bane's seven levels of feedback and had students create a page of notes with details about each level. With each piece of writing, they were responsible for deciding which level of feedback they wanted from the group. These notes would be their guide to both asking for and offering appropriate feedback.

Finally, I introduced the concept of the read-around. I brought out our talking piece—a polished granite egg. I told them that the egg represented the potential both in each piece of writing and in each of us. I told them that I wanted every person in the Circle to present something as the talking piece came around, even if it was the simplest thing. Some version of "the cat sat on the mat" would fulfill the requirement, if that was all they could offer. They should consider the talking piece permission to share their voice. I knew that I would never force someone to speak if they really could not, but I didn't offer passing as an option up-front. I really wanted students to commit to the process and to feel a sense of both permission and responsibility as a member of the writing Circle.

Before the writers presented a piece, they would tell us the title (if there was one), anything important they wanted us to know about the piece of writing (i.e., "I'm not as depressed as I sound in this poem, but it did help me work out some of my feelings"), and the level of feedback they were looking for. As each writer read their piece aloud, the other writers were to listen, follow along, and make notes on the hard copy they had in front of them. If we didn't have a copy of the piece being presented, I asked students to take notes, jot down key words, phrases, or ideas that stood out to them. At the end of the read-around, students would return these notes to the authors, providing them with a written log of feedback. These notes could be used in the rewriting process, or they could simply provide concrete affirmation of what worked well in the piece.

And so we began. My class sizes were small, usually between eight and fourteen students—an ideal size for a read-around Circle. Read-arounds work well with groups smaller than this, but when I had groups larger than fifteen, I would break the groups into two separate Circles and move between them. Generally, we could get through a read-around in two forty-five-minute class periods. Almost always, one or two writers would vie for the privilege of reading first. Following Circle guidelines, the talking piece would then move clockwise around the circle. This minimized the angst and drama over who would read next. If someone wanted to go last, he or she might try to sit strategically in the circle as we started, but once we started, the order was set.

Some students took to this new Circle format immediately. They loved the ritual of the talking piece and the simplicity of the form. A read-around Circle has no cross-talk or dialogue, so the writers are not allowed to answer questions, defend their piece of writing, or even express gratitude for positive feedback until the talking piece makes its way around the circle and back into their hands. In so many ways, we discovered, this freed us to listen, to build layers of meaning, to explore, and to uncover new ideas. Even the writers themselves would discover aspects or elements of the writing that they hadn't realized were there. In the past, a negative comment could have turned into an argument between a writer and a responder. But in the Circle, a criticism would almost always be diffused by the time the talking piece moved through more hands, adding more voices to the feedback.

Students began to compete to see who could offer the most original and intelligent-sounding analysis. They started to ask for terminology that would help them describe writing. I thus discovered the first organic method I had found for teaching literary terms. Once they had the language to talk about writing, they began to be more intentional about their own writing. Once they realized that Lindsay's writing was so powerful because she was so descriptive, suddenly students were filling their writing with details. The metaphors that Colin began using were so visual. Soon after, without any lecture on my part, metaphors and similes began cropping up in everyone's writing. I was no longer their sole teacher or audience, and they were no longer writing to placate me. They were also reading and analyzing more than they ever had in the past.

All the strong writing they were hearing prepared them to spot weak or rushed writing. I had taught them to start by looking for the strengths in a piece, and, incredibly, they almost always honored this. However, when they encountered a piece of writing that didn't feel honest or that had clearly been scratched out at the last second, they would often find kind but clear ways to say so and to suggest improvements. They would suggest, for example, that it would be nice to hear something next time that the writer really cared about. This was often enough to push the less engaged students to set the bar higher. It was a rare student who didn't eventually begin to write in earnest.

The culture in the classroom was now being driven by what happened in our read-around Circles. This culture respected stories, good writing, and honesty. They began to come to me with the books they were reading, noting where writers were making interesting choices, using wonderful descriptions, or even failing to live up to their ever-higher standards for good writing.

Students who were hesitant to buy in to the read-around still participated and contributed, even when they didn't put forward their best effort. Some of the teens who walked into my classroom hadn't attended a formal school in years. Others were one step away from being locked up. They battled addictions, violence, neglect, or anger every day of their lives. And yet every one of them would sit in Circle, say something to the other writers, and present something they had written.

One young woman, terrified to speak out loud, found that her hands shook so hard she couldn't read her piece of writing. Finally, her friend offered to hold it for her. She started out reading, "*The cat sat on the pink mat.*" The next time, she offered, "*The cat sat on the green mat in the sun.*" Read-around after read-around, month after month, she would listen, shaking, until she had read her piece, and then sit quietly dazed, soaking up others stories.

One day, as I checked in with her about what she was working on, she held up four pages of notebook paper, filled past the margins, and confessed that she was writing her autobiography. Each day, I watched as more pages were filled. When it came time for her to decide what she wanted to present, she asked how many pages were appropriate to share in one read-around. We settled on three pages, and she struggled for an entire class period deciding which three she wanted us to hear first.

The day she presented her first real piece of writing, she left half of her classmates in tears. She shared stories that, she confessed, she had never told anyone before. Through months of participating in the read-around, she realized that this was a safe place and that her peers would honor her story. Most profoundly, the others in the Circle recognized the gift she was offering to them. They were moved and grateful for the trust she had placed in them.

Time after time, I watched students take the risk of revealing a heretofore-unseen side of themselves in the read-around Circle. The seventeen-year-old slasher-writer gloried in watching everyone squirm as he described dismembered body parts. But then he would shock us all with his heartbreaking lyrics about the girl who would never be his. The class clown who reveled in his reputation as the boy with the lowest GPA read a poem about his longing for his father's approval. One young man had witnessed his father murder his mother and had not done one single academic task in the five months he was in school with us. Suddenly, he came forth with a poem from the point of view of a bug smashed on a windshield as a metaphor for how he felt about his life.

"I never, ever would have guessed that you had this side to you" became a regular refrain in our read-around Circles. I often asked students for permission to share their writing with other teachers on staff. I knew that seeing this other side of their students would help them work with the students more effectively and understand them more deeply.

The power of the read-around was contagious. The math teacher came to me to ask if I could encourage students to leave their writing notebooks in my classroom during math class, because students kept passing poetry back and forth under the table when they were meant to be working on balancing equations. I had a call from the halfway house, where fifteen of our students lived, saying that students were meeting in the bathrooms after lights-out to practice reading their poetry to each other in preparation for the coming day's read-around.

One student took his work to an open mic at a local coffeehouse and convinced one of his talented peers to come and admire his work there. She came along, brought her own work, and blew the audience away. She ended up on the Minnesota Poetry Slam team, traveling around performing spoken word pieces. He was somewhat disgruntled at this turn of events, but he made sure everyone knew that he was responsible for her being "discovered."

I decided to offer an elective class, after school, where students could come with work they had done outside of class and participate in a read-around. It was so popular I added a second class.

As I have moved to new schools, I have brought the read-around model with me. Each time, we have introduced the regular check-in Circle into the school community first as a way to establish the concept of the Circle, reinforce the norms, and build a sense of identity and trust. In the large public school where I currently teach, I have introduced the check-in Circle in my classroom as part of our Monday and Friday ritual to begin and end the week. In each setting, I have witnessed some students who plunge in, immediately producing crafted pieces of writing, and others who begin tentatively, one word at a time, perhaps waiting months before they realize what they have to say and that they are capable of sharing. In every case, their stories, their feedback, their honesty, and the Circle itself have transformed my classroom. As a teacher, I recognize the many ways that read-around Circles help me teach to the standards and enrich the curriculum I provide to my students. As a human being, I understand that this is a rare, precious, and vitally important thing.

Espanol en Circulo (Spanish in Circle)

Brenda Romereim

Brenda Romereim is a Spanish teacher and sports coach in Breckenridge, Minnesota. Breckenridge is a small town of 3,559 people

Brenda Romereim's Spanish class likes to sit in Circle, in part because they can see each other's faces, not the back of their heads. In this class, they can see each other's bubbles, which they then describe in Spanish. Photo by Brenda Romereim.

in a county that raises soybeans, corn, barley, and wheat. This school district has 830 students (91 percent White, 6 percent Latino or Chicano, and 2 percent Black or Native) and is located on the Minnesota–North Dakota border. The staff at her school was introduced to Circles as a process to use during homeroom advisory.

Brenda then started using the process in her Spanish class and on the softball field. As a coach, she held Circles both before and after each girls softball game, using the softball as the talking piece. Before the game, team members shared what they wanted to work on during the game. At the end—win or lose—they reflected on how well they did in developing the skill on which they focused. She uses the Circle process in her Spanish class to

Photos by Brenda Romereim.

engage the students, to ensure that everyone is speaking Spanish during class, and to provide students with opportunities for academic choices and decision-making.

I learned about her use of Circles from the person who trained her, Cindy Skalsky. I was looking for innovative uses of Circle, and Cindy told me about the softball Circle. Brenda and her Spanish students kindly responded to questions and a survey about Circles, and I have participated in workshops that Brenda presents regarding her classroom Circles.

If you sit in Brenda's class, you may see one, two, or even three talking pieces—mostly plastic animal shapes, like a dinosaur or gecko, or a stress ball—moving around the room. With two talking pieces, one student says a sentence in Spanish, and the student with the other talking piece—on the other side of the Circle—translates. Using three talking pieces, one student may ask a question in Spanish, another answers in Spanish, and the third person holding a talking piece translates both question and answer into English.

On other occasions, Brenda may have students stand in an inner and outer circle and ask each other questions that she has developed to help the students prepare for a test. The students in the inside circle pose the questions, which the students in the outside circle answer as best they can. If they give the wrong answer, then they receive the correct answer immediately. Then the outer circle shifts one person over and on to a new question. After a complete rotation, the students in the inside circle change places with those in the outside circle, and they have to answer questions. The circles provide order, and the standing gives students a chance to use their whole body in learning. They can move and get a little exercise, and they have some variety from the routine of rows.

Using the Circle process, Brenda also gives students opportunities to make academic choices. Students may set some of the standards for class projects as well as expectations for themselves

Breckenridge High School students in Circle. Photo by Brenda Romereim.

and for her. For instance, in Circle, the class sets the criteria for a Spanish-language newscast. Brenda sends the talking piece around, asking each student to offer one criterion that should be used to grade students on their group project. She (or a student) writes the criterion on a blackboard or poster paper. Various components might be offered—a weather report, a human interest story, or a sports report. "It will have to be in Spanish," one student offers. "Yeah, and Ms. Romereim wants correct pronunciation." Lighting, camera shots, set design, and time length for segments are all added to the list. Humor might be good; costumes could make it interesting; or an interview with the superintendent could give it standing. Sentence structure, grammar, as well as theme music go on the list. Then the talking piece goes around again, and the students vote on their top two or three criteria. Brenda maintains the teacher's prerogative for Spanish, grammar, and pronunciation, but the students select the other criteria for grading. As the teacher, of course, Brenda could make up the rubric for the group project. However, this collaborative process takes about the same amount of time, and it is much more engaging for students.

Brenda responded to some questions about her work with Circle.

Why did you start using the Circle in your classroom in the first place?

I started using Circles in my classroom as an experiment. I had attended a short presentation on the basics of Circles and decided to try it in my classroom. I felt this could be my solution to participation problems in Spanish class. The Circle provided a better means of engaging all students and increasing their participation. I use it for many topics now.

I also struggled with getting information back to students in a timely manner. Using the Circle gave me an opportunity to offer immediate feedback.

What do you like about the process as a teacher?

I have learned that students enjoy the opportunity to hear everyone speak. Plus, I can give feedback to students immediately after an activity or assignment using the Circle. I have used the Circle to practice and review for tests, as well as to learn from the results. I have used Circles as a means for students to create projects. Students use the Circle to decide what will be necessary in the project and how the project will be graded. Circles have allowed me to become a better teacher and to improve my weaknesses. They also create student-directed learning. I now see students using the Circle by themselves in my classroom. Circles have helped me be creative and learn from my students. In my opinion, I could use Circles to do just about anything in my classroom.

What are the Circle's limitations, if any?

Large groups are hard to keep focused. I also need to limit the time in a class period, so a Circle isn't too long. If it runs too long, students lose interest, and we don't accomplish much. Some students have difficulty waiting to speak. The teacher has to be enthusiastic about the process to make it work. The teacher also needs to clarify the rules early on, and then it seems to work.

One of my Spanish II classes described the Circle process in my class:

- Move desks to get organized. Use a talking piece. Have a subject, topic, or theme.
- The Circle is less formal. It provides active learning.
- Students lead. Standing Circles. No homework. Teacher has the grade book.
- Outside-of-classroom Circles in the gym or outdoors.
- Circles are more open, easier to understand, and help in learning from others.

To assess how her students were responding to Circles, Brenda made an informal survey of the students in her Spanish II class. The students used the Circle daily, and they noted several benefits and some challenges of talking and listening in Spanish. One student wrote that she liked "hearing everyone individually, and you feel more connected in a Circle. Then we usually get on a good, important subject and learn things we didn't know before. Circles help everyone get a chance to say something, and each class should take a few minutes to use it."

While all this is the boon of Circles, the bane for some students is that they have to talk. This is the very reason Brenda uses it—to be sure that everyone is, as one student wrote, "being put on the spot—but it helps." Another wrote, "When it's my turn to speak, I stress a little over what to say to make sure it (the Spanish) sounds right or relatable." Another commented, "You are no longer in your comfort zone. It makes us use Spanish, puts us on the spot . . . but that's life."

Other students reported that the Circle enhanced their learning process:

- "I think it helps me learn more easily and puts me in a less stressful situation, because I'm not totally on my own. I get to literally see everyone else learning also."
- "We learn together and make mistakes together. Watching others make mistakes helps me not only learn from my own but also from theirs."
- "You get to interact with other students, and that (makes it) easier to pay attention and learn than when we're being lectured to."
- "It does make me use Spanish. It can be fun, and we get to talk more as a class; it is more interesting."

The physical layout of Circle appealed to several students, particularly "being able to see other people's faces," as one student wrote. Another expanded on this idea: "I like activities, creating our own story going around the circle. I like it because it is different from just sitting in our desks facing forward. It doesn't seem like you are in a classroom when you're facing everyone else." Other students commented: "It brings every person to an equal table. No one can hide," and "I like how we all get to participate and that everything moves smoothly. I also like that we can see everybody else."

Several students noted that, in Circle, they were able to learn from each other. Circle "involves everyone, and it is an easy way to tell who understands"—"to see what everyone's point of view

Students speak in Spanish as they pass the purple shark talking piece around. Everyone can see the speaker, and everyone has a chance to practice the language as the talking piece goes around the Circle in order. Photo by Brenda Romereim.

is." In the Spanish II class, one student wrote, "It allows us to hear our classmates' questions and learn from how other students answer them. It is a way to put our knowledge to use." Another student noted the benefits to the teacher: "Circles in our school are very helpful. You learn a lot because you get to listen to other people and hear their questions. It is also helpful for the teacher, because she has to answer a question only once."

The students recognized that Circles do not work if people do not honor the talking piece, which means there are "too many side conversations, lack of attention (which happens very rarely)." Another student reported that outbursts of feelings can sidetrack the Circle: "Sometimes a Circle would get very noisy when we would be talking about something exciting and then we would get off track." The antidote is to follow the process: "I like how we pass something around and only the person with it can talk."

Talking pieces are chosen to reflect the interests of the participants and the focus of a Circle. Brenda's talking pieces range from stuffed dinosaurs to plastic lizards, a small ball to a hacky sack, and Beanie Babies to playdough.

Students were also asked if they would use Circles outside of school. Many said they would and did. Students could see themselves using Circles for talking to friends, for a meeting, at a youth group, or at Girl Scouts. A few students had used the process in other settings, such as volleyball team Circles and "for our Rotary group." "I participate in discussions," one student wrote, "and oftentimes we fight to get our input in. I mentioned the idea of taking turns, and we are able to solve the task much more efficiently." "If I was grouped with people I don't know," another student wrote, "it would be a good way to get to know everyone."

CHAPTER 7

Teaching with Intention

Circle Activities in the Classroom

The norm for communication in most classrooms is that you raise your hand when you want to speak. I was one of those students who had her hand up all the time, whether I had an answer or not. I just wanted to be called on. If the teacher called on me and I didn't know the answer, I would just make something up. I did not understand why everyone didn't raise his or her hand every time. It never dawned on me that some people actually think before they speak! The Circle process gives quiet students permission to talk and extroverted students (like me) permission to practice self-control and to take time to think.

What does it mean to make Circle processes the norm for communication in a classroom? What does that look like? Of course, one does not have to use Circles all the time; this is not practical or necessary. Students of all ages need to learn how to navigate many different methods of communication. But the Circle process can enhance learning in formal and informal educational settings. Consider the following ways that educators and student support staff have used the process.

Three-Minute Music Circles

Kathy is an elementary music teacher who works in a small rural school district. Her day consists of twenty-five minute classes, one right after the other, with fifteen to twenty-five students per class. There is no passing time; when she opens the door to let one class out, the next class is standing along the wall waiting to come in. Luckily for the music teacher, the students are versed in the Circle process, because their classroom teachers use Circles for daily morning meeting.

When they come into her music room, the students immediately sit in circle on the floor. Kathy sits with them, welcomes them to class, and asks them to focus on the music class by sitting in silence for one minute. During those sixty seconds, Kathy catches her breath and organizes the class in her mind. Then she sends the talking piece around, a large plastic black eighth-note, asking the students to say their name and, in one word, to share how they are feeling today. This gives her the chance to see each student, hear their voice, hear a little about how they were feeling, and bring their focus to her. Taking the two minutes for this go-round gives Kathy a full twenty-two minutes to spend on music with a focused class.

Social Studies Class and HIV

Angela Wilcox, the language arts and social studies teacher who developed read-arounds, also uses Circles to introduce a new unit. Before she outlines the material to be covered, she asks the students what they know about the topic. The go-around with the talking piece provides her with an informal assessment of knowledge, which sometimes reveals an unexpected resource. The HIV/AIDS unit in her social studies class was a case in point.

As the talking piece went around the tenth and eleventh graders, Angela heard misconceptions ("Only gay people get AIDS"), nuggets of fact ("You can't get AIDS by shaking hands with someone with HIV"), and a few disrespectful comments about people with AIDS ("It's their own fault if they get it, right?"). Then a quiet girl who rarely spoke took the talking piece and said, "I know something about this disease. My foster sister has HIV. She got it when she was born. She is ten now. She didn't do anything to get it, she isn't gay, and she is pretty healthy." Immediately, the tone of the discussion changed. The topic went from another social study unit to a specific human experience. On several occasions as the class studied the epidemic, students would turn to the girl and ask for her knowledge and her opinion.

Transitions in the Classroom

A behavior specialist in a Minneapolis K–8 school, Jack Mangan, used Circles in the classroom to help students deal with transitions. For many elementary school students, their connection to their teacher is profound, and some students respond poorly to changes in routine, such as the sudden absence of a teacher-due to illness or a teacher leaving the class in the middle of the year. Mangan helped students manage each situation with the Circle process. Taking the time for these transition Circles with students ultimately saves him time in his office later on dealing with individual students who were upset about the change in teachers.

For example, Mangan would use a transition Circle when a teacher left school in the middle of the year due to a pregnancy. On the teacher's last day, he would convene a Circle that included the substitute teacher. He would ask the students, "Share one thing that you have learned from your teacher." His question for the next round was, "What do you hope to learn from your new teacher? What could you commit to doing to help the class work together with your new teacher?" Finally, he asked, "Is there anything you want to say to your teacher before she leaves to have her baby?" At the end of the Circle, the teacher made some closing remarks, got up, and gave the class talking piece to the substitute teacher, showing the transfer of care and responsibility.

Mangan advises Circle keepers to bring a box of Kleenex for this type of Circle—"Usually, everyone is bawling at the end."

The Class That Ate the Substitute Teacher

Mangan has also used Circles to repair any harm that a class has inflicted on a substitute teacher. When a class has become disruptive and unruly to a sub, Mangan would invite the substitute to return to the school the next day and meet with the regular teacher and the class in Circle.

Mangan would tell the students and teachers why he was there: "Yesterday, in Room 227, there was difficulty with learning. The principal was called to the classroom twice. Two students were sent to my office. Ms. Yang, your teacher, has never sent a student to my office this year. So, Ms. Yang and I asked Ms. Jacobs, your substitute teacher, to come back to class so we can talk about what happened, figure out if there is anything that needs to be fixed, and to make a plan so that learning can happen all the time. I have brought the feather. We know that when the feather is messed up, the bird cannot fly. Let us try to smooth out the feather as we talk."

Through rounds in Circle, he would then invite the students and the teachers to reflect on the following basic questions:

- What happened yesterday in this classroom?
- What were you thinking at the time?
- What can be done to make a substitute teacher's visit a good learning experience for everyone?
- Is there anything anyone would like to say?

To close the Circle, Mangan would invite everyone to stand, make the circle smaller, and hand the talking piece to the class's regular teacher, who would offer some positive closing remarks.

By doing this, Mangan was able to keep a steady roster of substitute teachers on whom the school could depend to come in and teach. When a substitute was asked to attend such a Circle, the principal agreed to pay the substitute a half-day's wages for his or her time, as she knew it was a good investment. Having substitutes that a principal can count on and who know the school, the staff, and eventually many students is just easier for everyone. It provides some degree of continuity to students in a situation that is, by nature, disruptive.

Helping a Class Recover

Sometimes an entire class can seem to take a turn for the worse: snippy comments there, exclusion on the playground here, mean-mugging done by different students at different times at a "target," or "marking" one student for everyone to pick on. Instead of investigating who said what when, teachers turned to Mangan for help in these instances. He would respond with a more global intervention, which sometimes meant something as simple as going to the class and reading a book. One of his favorites was *Puppies for Sale*, a picture storybook about a boy who wanted to buy a puppy that had a disability, a weak back leg.[1] Mangan wrote:

> We like to combine the Circle process and quality literature to promote ethical character development. When we present a book with a moral value, we use a process promoted by Dr. William Glasser. The process states the first step is to generalize the value, then personalize the value, and finally challenge the group to embrace the value as their own.
>
> The first pass around the circle, we ask the children, "What is teasing?" The second time we ask the students to tell of a time when they were teased. Finally, we challenge the children by asking them, "Next time you see someone

being teased, what are you going to do?" We then ask the
teacher to close the Circle.[2]

SEAD: Stop Everything and Dialogue

Dr. Dee Lundell worked for more than thirty years as an elementary school teacher and special education director in Minneapolis. For the 2001–2003 school years, her K–8 school
received funding to implement restorative measures. The staff
was trained in the Circle process by Cordelia Anderson and was
encouraged to use it in their classrooms on a daily basis. Lundell
and Anderson led a group of teachers and aides in developing
activities that combined restorative philosophy with other classroom management practices.

"It is just a better day," Lundell said, "if you stay in that restorative way." Indeed, the school she worked at experienced a significant drop in suspensions as the students and teachers got to
know each other better through Circles. In reality, teachers were
not always able to conduct their morning meetings in Circle;
other demands sometimes disrupted their regular routine. Nonetheless, the planning team developed a monthly plan of activity
that encouraged daily Circle time called SEAD: Stop Everything
and Dialogue. SEAD combined social skills lessons, discussion
groups, art activities, and a school-wide promotion campaign for
SEAD and Circles. Lundell described it in a grant report:

> Monthly school-wide Circle dialogues occur when staff
> select topics, such as positive and negative peer pres-
> sure, "Keys to a Peaceable Kingdom: what would your
> classroom look like or sound like if it were peaceful," or
> bullying, etc. Every classroom in the school has a Circle
> dialogue; then the students—in small groups or individu-
> ally—make some art—a poster, poem, or picture that
> represents ideas expressed in the Circle. The art is then

posted in the hallways, so everyone can be reminded of
the topic and of the positive actions that can be done to
make schools safe.[3]

On the first Monday of each month, the entire school stopped
everything and dialogued on a topic related to the school climate. The staff and the student council took turns selecting the
topic, such as respect, bullying, giving and receiving, friendship,
or cooperation. Both groups remained flexible on their topic selection, so they could address hot issues in the school whenever
they came up. The SEAD team developed three or four questions
for the topic, and this "lesson plan" was given to each classroom.

Prompts for the Circle—questions such as Jack Mangan
used—bring the general topic into the Circle during a first round.
For a second round, the question gives participants an opportunity to personalize the issue and talk about how they might have
experienced it in their own lives. The third question challenges
participants to think about how they can contribute to the collective good. Additional questions can give students a chance to
talk about what they see the school doing to address a problem
or to promote the health of the community. Some people want
to talk about "the system" before talking about what they per-
sonally can do for the good of the group. Such discussions about
"what the school does well or poorly" also provide adults with
insight and may even reveal new areas of concern.

Here is a sample set of questions that SEAD uses for the
school-community Circles to explore issues around respect:

- What do you think respect means?
- Describe a time when you showed someone respect.
- What does it feel like when people are disrespectful?
- If you want, share a time when you felt disrespected.
- What does the school do well to show respect to all
  the people here?

- What could the school do better?
- What suggestions do you have for the principal?
- What can you do to show respect in this school?

Another sample topic for SEAD is bus safety. Here are some keeper prompts to help students describe a safe bus:

- What does a good, safe bus—
    look like?
    sound like?
    feel like?
    smell like?
- What are some ideas of actions we could take to have a good, safe bus?
- What do you agree to do to make the bus a good place for everybody?

Of course, these questions could be adapted to prompt dialogue about safety in the lunchroom, hallway, or playground.

To follow up and reinforce the Circle dialogue, SEAD keepers divide students into groups of four or five. Then they invite them to make a poster that illustrates the Circle discussion. Through art, they depict the ideas generated—perhaps one of the Circle agreements about being respectful, for example.

By putting up the artwork, writings, posters, or a list of the role-play titles or skits, each class in the school helps to "market" or promote positive behavior. As students and staff move through the hallways, they can see visual representations of what people discussed about topics like "respect" or "friendship." They can see the school-wide efforts to make a better school. Holding the Circles every month and then changing the posters in the hallway to reflect the new dialogue helps to keep the momentum fresh and vital.[4]

Circles to Discuss Challenging Topics

Cordelia Anderson has worked on many prevention projects as a consultant and writer. One major initiative was the State of Minnesota's violence prevention mass media campaign called "You're The One Who Can Make The Peace." One of the tools she developed for the campaign was a one-page description of how to use Circles to discuss challenging topics.[5]

Horrific public events—a school shooting, a natural disaster, or the attacks of 9/11—affect a school and may engender fear in both students and adults. Adults may prefer not to talk about the news. However, part of creating an environment conducive to learning involves adults using these difficult situations as teachable moments.

Learning does not happen in a climate of fear, anxiety, rumor, and confusion. Yet students may be hard pressed to bring up topics when the nonverbal message they get from adults is, "We are not going to deal with this." Using social skills, such as speaking and listening, adults can help students, themselves, and other adults address their feelings enough so that everyone can focus on learning.

Anderson encourages using Circles to help students process such events. The opening can be as simple as, "How many of you heard the news this morning?" This question can be followed with, "What do we know?" "What don't we know?" "How do we feel?" And, "What can we do to help each other?" Having discussions in Circle ensures that all voices will be heard: the ill-informed and unaware, the scared, the ones who need help, and the ones who can help.

As people talk, the keeper might frame questions that

- encourage people to discuss what they have heard. This helps students learn how to separate what is known from rumor.

- allow students to put words to their feelings around the situation. Naming feelings helps students and adults move from the part of the brain that experiences emotions to the part that holds the executive, decision-making functions. The executive part of our brains generates options for how we respond to our emotions.
- identify resources. Whom can students go to for help in the school, in the community, and in their family? Youth and children need to take time to identify formal and informal supports. Some students may be able to rattle off a number of adults whom they trust and who might be able to help them. Hearing these options may give ideas to other students who may have felt that they have few or no helping adults in their lives.
- brainstorm positive steps that students can take. One antidote to fear is action. Knowing some concrete actions that individuals can take instills a sense of power and purpose. This is especially true for children and youth who may feel overwhelmed by the larger forces of life. Brainstorming positive steps may also introduce alternatives for students who may have started to act in a negative way.

In other words, through the prompting questions posed for a Circle round, keepers can challenge students to help, to be supportive, and to take action.

When the subject involves emotions, it's especially beneficial that the adults in the Circle can easily see all the students as they take the talking piece, one by one. This allows the adult to more readily assess not only what student say but also how they look. Students who seem particularity upset or withdrawn may appreciate being offered the opportunity to talk with the student support staff.

Morning meeting in Circle. Photo courtesy of the St. Croix Valley Restorative Justice Program.

High School Discussion Mornings

Anderson adapted the basic Circle process for large-scale discussions in a number of ways. In one instance, the staff at a high school wanted to address issues of racism. The administrators asked her for help. After meeting with the staff and some students, Anderson realized that the students felt that racism was not the only issue affecting the climate of the school. Additional issues were surfacing: bullying, harassment, disrespect. They suggested, for example, shifting the norm for bystanders from "not" (not my job, not my responsibility, not my business) to an expectation to become involved: when you know of harm, take some action to help.

She trained students on bystander issues, and the students put together a fifteen-minute video that aired school-wide. She also trained the students to keep Circles. In Circles, they each posed the same questions about the bystander role and how the school community might move in a more positive direction.

The Circle discussions about race, school climate, and bystander expectations took place in the lunchroom of a large suburban high school. The lunchroom was set up to accommodate over one thousand juniors in Circles at the same time. The adults were peppered throughout the room, convinced they would need to step in to keep the process going and the students focused. With the student Circle keepers grounded and prepared, and one student talking at a time, according to Circle protocol, the room was humming with focus and respectful dialogue.

The adults—staff, teachers, administrators—had nothing to do, so Anderson held a Circle for them. The discussion revealed the need for more restorative work among the staff. They were carrying multiple tensions that they had not yet discussed openly.

For both the students and the staff, the Circle questions included the following:

- What kinds of harmful behaviors are you most aware of happening in the school?
- Are certain individuals or groups viewed by some as okay to disregard, look down on, or hate?
- Do most students or adults speak up or take action to help when they see harmful behaviors?
- What stops you from helping or makes it hard for you to take action?
- What can the school or you do to move things forward in a positive way?

Like the idea of SEAD, these Circle discussions can serve as a springboard for further actions. The school community might develop a media campaign within the school to build mutual acceptance and respect. Or, perhaps a task force could discuss the school recommendations with the administrators or make a request for further education or programming. Identifying the problem in an inclusive process is just a first step.[6] Circles can be used with school staff as well, Anderson points out, to deal with staff-to-staff, staff-to-administrators, and staff-to-parent conflicts. "Staff can also benefit," Anderson says, "from building community, strengthening relationships, and addressing conflict."

Individual Education Plans and Restorative Principles

The first version of using Circles for Individual Education Plans for special education students that I heard of was done by an assistant principal in a K–8 school. She used a talking piece that held some meaning for the particular student and that the parent(s) brought in. To remind everyone that the student they were discussing was more than test scores and referral reports, the assistant principal encouraged the choice of a favorite toy, pictures of the student in a baseball uniform, or stuffed animals to serve as talking pieces. In one instance, I do believe the talking piece was a five-foot stuffed Tweety Bird!

Using the Circle process helps to establish a sense of equality among the participants. It also helps everyone recognize each participant's formal and informal knowledge on the topic. The talking piece organizes the communication, bringing balance to the voices in the room. Using the four components of the process—meeting and getting acquainted; building understanding and trust; addressing the vision and issues; and developing plans and a sense of unity—provides a structure that starts with everyone's strengths and assets.

The Minnesota Department of Education provided Circle trainings for the state's special education mediators. For them, it was another practice to use in addition to their mediation skills, as a situation suggested it. Many of the special education mediators, who provide mediation services to school districts and parents, were already cross-trained in restorative justice practices, either in Circles, conferencing, or both.

Staff Meeting Ideas

Tracy Olson, who works in an alternative learning program in Rochester, Minnesota, has used Circles with her staff in a number of ways.

For example, at the beginning of each staff meeting, she sends the talking piece around and asks staff members, "Name a student you appreciate today." The name is said without comment, but the effect is to help bring perspective to the meeting. Not everything is a mess at the school; not all students are having problems.

The meeting is then conducted in the usual way. At the end, Tracy takes up the talking piece again and asks for a closing comment: "How was the meeting for you?" "What will you do this evening for yourself?" "What are you looking forward to tomorrow?"

Each morning, fifteen minutes before the buses arrive, the staff circles up in the atrium of the school. The talking piece goes around once with a check-in question. Then the staff share announcements: "There is a field trip today"; "Check in with Mel—his mom is in the hospital"; or "Remember to get the forms in for the survey." The gathering serves the same purpose as a huddle: "What are we doing next?" In other words, "Let us look at each other and connect, because we need each other to make the play."

The school does a check-in and checkout Circle with the students in advisory on Mondays and Fridays: "How was the weekend?" and "What are you looking forward to doing this weekend?" This helps the teachers get a feel for how the students are doing after being away from the routine of school. It is also a way to show interest in and concern for all the students. The check-in and checkout Circles help the students share a bit of how they are feeling, and it promotes a little reflection and future thinking. It also gives the teachers an opportunity to share their concerns with both the students and the student support staff.

Restorative Guides in Schools

In 1998, the South St. Paul School District (SSP) received a grant to implement and evaluate restorative practices in the elementary, junior, and senior high schools. The district provided on-going training and coaching in the Circle process to teachers and other staff members. They also decided to hire "restorative guides." The guides were trained specifically to conduct Circles to repair harm, yet trouble did not occur every day. Nor did teachers immediately trust the guides to handle a fight between two of their students.

The guides used a variety of activities to develop connections with the students, staff, and teachers. Michael Stanefski and Mercy Adams were hired under the initial grant to South St. Paul and worked in the junior/senior high school and the elementary school, respectively. JoAnn Ward and Jodelle Ista were community members from the South St. Paul Community Justice Council. The Council created a pool of volunteers and later funded positions for Ward and Ista to work as guides in the elementary schools after the grant funding ended.

I asked the South St. Paul guides how they would build relations in the school. They first recommended that the guides be present—in the hallways, at parent-teacher conferences, at choir concerts, at school functions, or in the classroom. "Volunteer to supervise the lunchroom," Stanefski suggested. "When I was at SSP, this was a great way for me to meet students and get to know them in their own element. It is also a great way to 'mentor' the cafeteria staff in restorative ways to work with students, as a large part of their job is managing behavior." JoAnn Ward said, "Simply being present to listen (bear witness) to students can be powerful for them. It can lead to opportunities to strengthen healthy values, encourage healthy decision-making, and allow appropriate referrals to needed services that no one else knows are needed."

Mercy Adams recommended providing trainings: "Partner with community organizations to do workshops in classrooms—and with staff, of course!" Ward would "support staff in learning positive communications [RJ] skills" through workshops and role modeling. "Offer to provide classroom Circles of learning," she said, "as a way to think more deeply about a subject," such as social studies or literature. These learning Circles show teachers how to use Circles while giving them a break.

Ista identified the practical needs of a restorative guide: supportive literature (e.g., "Free Spirit Publishing has good information" on students' social and emotional needs[7]); a room in which to hold Circles; a computer; a phone; support from the administration; and a standing invitation to attend staff meetings. She also suggests supplies for Circle centerpieces, talking pieces, and activities: "Does the guide have pipe cleaners and beads for talking pieces? A few years ago, a trainer came to our school and displayed the talking piece her daughter had made out of pipe cleaners and beads. I had no clue what a soothing instrument a pipe cleaner could be, plus it opens up the creativity of the maker."[8]

Proactive Circles

A school counselor developed the use of "proactive Circles" to build community within the school and to build awareness of what different students might be experiencing. She wrote in an email:

> We used a proactive Circle at one of our high schools with a group of students from the different grade levels. Over the course of the year, we videotaped their

discussions about their experiences at the school. Then we used these video clips during school-wide "focus time" to generate all-school discussions about many issues: being new in school and finding your place, speaking a language other than English, what school pride/ spirit means, how to support each other, and who we look to for help. It was a powerful and valued experience, not only for the twelve students involved in the group, but also for many of the students in the school.

This use illustrates the power of Circles to generate positive, engaging discussions among students about shared values and experiences. Through the process, a sense of community builds, as students come to understand each other more from the inside out.

Circle Applications in Schools

"For some people in schools," wrote Cordelia Anderson, "Circles are a way of life. For others, a Circle is a circle is a circle." For the former, the Circle embodies a set of values that inform how they work with youth, colleagues, and family. For the latter, it is simply a practical communication process.

While Circles may at first seem to be just a communication technique, using them regularly over time reveals their potential to strengthen connections, to help people acknowledge each others' differences, and to support a group in moving forward in a good way. Circles honor the voices and perceptions of all involved, and this inevitably sends a positive message to individual participants as well as to the group as a whole. Students learn how to be together differently—in mutually supportive ways. Circles are a place for modeling respectful and compassionate behaviors, and, with time and Circle use, this experiential learning tends to carry over to how students behave even when they are not sitting (or standing) in Circle.

People who are new to Circles will most likely come up with ways that Circles can be used to prevent problems and to intervene when problems do occur in their own school environments. Certainly, longtime Circle practitioners in schools have been using Circles to teach class material as well as to build the social and emotional supports essential to student learning. Using Circles promotes strengths, assets, and protective factors within and among the participants. Many schools are now using Circles across the school community in a wide range of circumstances to address many needs for building—or restoring—good relations.

After more than a decade of teachers and administrators using Circles in Minnesota schools, the applications of Circles continues to evolve. The uses and benefits I describe in what follows are not meant to limit the possibilities but to stimulate the imagination.

Circles of Understanding

This use of Circles helps participants gain a new or deeper understanding of others in the Circle, whether the Circle is used with students, teachers, administrators, or a blending of these. Circles of understanding can be used for staff development, to help students get to know each other better, to glean new perspectives of others during a conflict, or to address diversity. Circles of understanding help participants slow down and open up to the perceptions, insights, and needs of others.

Dialogue Circles, Talking Circles, or Topic Circles

These Circles allow participants to talk about how they perceive a topic or issue or how outcomes or directions have affected them. The topics can be curriculum related, or they can be related to current issues weighing on people's minds (war, policy changes, cuts, elections, dress codes, etc.).

Lesson Circles

A wide variety of teachers (such as math, science, writing, literature, history, civics, social studies, health) use a Circle at the beginning of a lesson to allow students to share their knowledge, perceptions, ideas, and concerns related to the lesson. Circles can also be used at the end of a unit as a review for a test or to allow students to reflect on the unit and its impact on them. In these Circles, students have a chance to offer their feedback to the teacher about classroom activities and lessons.

Healing Circles

After a crisis, trauma, or harm has occurred, Circles provide a safe, reflective place for staff, students, families, and the community to talk about what happened, to share how they were affected by the conflict or harm, to express their needs, and to offer ideas about how to move forward in a positive way. Circles have been used to give students, teachers, and staff processing time after student suicides, sudden death, accidents, and other traumas.

Seminar Circles

In the usual lecture format, an expert gives a class or group direction, information, and consultation. Circles change the format. In enrichment or advanced programs, Circles give students a way to gain insights from peers and to learn from each other.

Circles for Intervening on Problematic Behaviors and for Repairing Harm

Using a Circle to deal with harmful behaviors or violations requires an experienced, trained Circle keeper and more preparation. The keeper(s) needs to identify likely participants, invite and prepare them, and then consider whatever monitoring or follow-up may be necessary. While some teachers or administrators may call a Circle to respond to trouble on the spot, more planning and preparation may be necessary when problems have festered or when the harm is severe and more complex.

Conflict Circles

These Circles allow the individuals in a conflict, along with others affected by the conflict, to come together to share perspectives, needs, and ideas. These Circles also require a trained keeper and preparation.

Circles for Re-entry

After a student has been suspended, this type of Circle brings together the student, the student's family, the core teacher, and an administrator to provide a show of support for the student, to make a plan to change problematic behavior, and to repair harm. Some schools encourage students to participate in a Circle held partway into a suspension, especially if either the student or the school staff have a restitution plan they want to present to potentially shorten the length of suspension.

Circles for Individual Education Plans (IEP)

When an IEP meeting is held in Circle, the participants and the purpose of the IEP meeting remain the same, but the use of the talking piece can help bring a sense of equality to the process. Introverts are encouraged to speak, and extroverts are provided the opportunity to listen. The selection of a talking piece that represents the student in question can keep the student ever-present, even though the student may not be physically in the room.

Truancy Circles

In one community, the truancy Circle consisted of the student's family members, school staff, and personnel from the human services agency, who came to provide information and resources if needed. In another community, the truancy Circle consisted of elders who met twice a month at the school to discuss attendance issues with students and family members. In both Circles, the emphasis was on support and problem solving, so the student got back to class.

Writing Circles

There are many variations on writing Circles. Students can be encouraged to strengthen their writing skills by doing individual writing and then sharing aspects of their work in Circle. Circles can also help students gather ideas for writing.

Circles for Staff Development or Classroom Connections

These Circles are used to strengthen relationships, increase mutual understanding, problem solve, and build communication. They may occur at set intervals of time (weekly, monthly), such as during advisory sessions.

Circles—Ongoing

A set time for an ongoing Circle can afford staff or students an opportunity to drop in to a regularly held Circle. The basic intention of the Circle could be to provide support, to create an opportunity to discuss current issues, or to simply be a place for participants to connect with each other. An ongoing Circle in a school may also enable experienced Circle members to help the administration by being the community of care for a student who may have been harmed or who may need to repair harm. Ongoing Circles can also invite administrators to come in and provide perspectives on school issues, much as a student council does.

There are excellent books available on the Circle process. They provide deep insight into the history, process, and possibility of Circles, especially as a restorative process to address harms, conflicts, or crimes. Circles are now being used to repair many kinds of harms that commonly occur in schools, from addressing fights to peeling back the complexity of bullying to helping a class repair the harm done to a substitute teacher. Conducting such Circles requires care, knowledge, and training.

Repairing harm in a restorative way often means inviting a victim, a person who caused harm, and other affected parties to a face-to-face meeting. However, as much promise as the process holds, it can also result in causing more harm. Experiential training, coaching, mentorship as well as participating in Circles focused on repairing harm are recommended ways of learning how to use the process for such challenging situations. Training helps Circle keepers conduct these Circles in ways that lower the risk of negative consequences. Keepers learn how Circles can hold participants on a constructive, respectful path, even while dealing with personal pain.

CHAPTER 8

Using Circles to Repair Harm

Using Circles in school to teach or to help build community does not require significant training, although I highly recommend an experiential Circle training of two to four days as a start. However, as I said at the close of the previous chapter, using the Circle process to repair harm or in lieu of a suspension requires additional training. Knowledge of restorative practices, the dynamics of victims and offenders, and the deeper philosophy and practices of Circles vastly expand Circle keeping skills. In schools, it is particularly important for keepers to be versed in the dynamics of bullying. And their work is greatly enhanced when they have some knowledge of the theory of restorative principles, especially regarding shame, humiliation, and empathy.

To illustrate how Circles have been used to repair harms, here are some stories.

A Senior High Fight

As adolescents grow into adulthood, they move from a self-centered view of the world to a perspective that encompasses both self and others, youth development researcher Gisela Konopka notes. Youth do all kinds of things that provide exceptional opportunities for self-reflection and for taking a wider perspective. The discussions in a Circle can be profound, as the following story from a high school aide illustrates.

Four juniors got into a fight in the school hallway. They were sent to the office and, in lieu of suspension, agreed to sit in Circle to try to repair the harm. Three boys admitted to jumping the fourth boy because he had made disparaging remarks about a friend of theirs who had been killed in a car crash earlier in the month. Through discussion, all four boys agreed that the person they had harmed the most was the boy who had died. He did not deserve the disparaging remarks, and he would not have wanted his friends to start a fight. So, they all agreed to go to the cemetery and, one by one, to apologize to the dead boy at his grave.

These boys may have struggled with conflicting values: defending a dead friend's honor versus honest speech, however insensitive. They also were experimenting with their own identity. For example, by fighting, am I brave, a true friend, or a tough kid? By talking out loud, am I painfully honest, clever with words, mean, unthinking, or a bully? What is my relationship to my friends, to the school, and, in this instance, to the dead? They tried out several roles in the course of this story, right up to the visit to the gravesite.

The alternative consequence to the Circle for all four of the boys would have been out-of-school suspension. Their feelings of grief, anger, or shame may go unaddressed. Spending three to five days isolated at home would do little to "encourage reflection on self in relation to others or self-discovery by looking outward as well as inward," as these boys did.[1]

Disorderly Conduct and Dancing

Although most people think that dancing expresses joy in life, at one high school and with one group of girls, a discussion about different dance styles and the girls' dancing abilities resulted in an argument. The argument went from the hall to the bus. It drew a crowd, and finally, the police liaison officer was called in to handle the situation. The officer could have charged the girls with disorderly conduct. In addition, the assistant principal could have suspended them from school for two to three days. Instead, they all agreed to meet in Circle and to develop an agreement.

At the core of the shouting was the issue of respect. "One student perceived another student to be talking about her and disrespecting her way of dancing," wrote the social worker who facilitated the Circle. The girls—Tsehai, Samantha, Kee, Zoie, and Tanisha—were African American, Hmong American, African immigrant, and Anglo. The last two girls were the arguers, and both were transfer students, one from Kenya, the other from inner-city Boston.

Part of the issue among the four students was the different levels of experience and comfort in dancing. As the new kids in the school, two of the girls were vying for attention by displaying their clear talent for dancing. In the Circle discussion, however, the girls realized they had more in common with each other than not. All the girls were able to "quickly acknowledge they were really coming from the same place, same style of dance," and could share in each other's experiences. The agreement was that they would repair the harm by coming together in the hallway for a "shared dance experience after school."

In evaluating a process, restorative practitioners look to assess both the intended and the unintended outcomes. The photos that were taken of the dance session showed girls who seemed to be participating in creative arts, learning self-expression, and cultivating a capacity to enjoy life—all intended outcomes and in line with Konopka's positive youth development. In this instance, an unintended but positive outcome, at least from the teenage girls' perspectives, was that some boys stopped by to watch and cheer them on.

A Principal's Appalling Behavior

At the start of a workshop week, a principal found his keys missing from his desk. He was furious and turned his anger on new staff members, accusing them of theft. The response to the lost keys seemed out of proportion, and the staff members were appalled that he had acted so accusingly toward the new teachers. The school had a restorative justice planner, and the staff members asked him to call a Circle with the principal. The planner met with the principal, and he agreed to sit in Circle with the staff members who were most upset or worried about the incident.

In the course of the Circle, the principal revealed—perhaps for the first time, it seemed—that early in his career, his keys were stolen. The thief had broken into his office, trashed his desk, and left animal feces on his chair. This incident triggered his recent response to the lost keys (they had been found) and explained some of his overreaction. He apologized. In response, Circle participants expressed their concern that he had had such a demeaning experience. Staff members, both old and new, appreciated his honesty. What could have been an incident that clouded the entire school year was acknowledged in its entirety. Unexpectedly, some long-standing issues for the principal were addressed. Not only could the whole incident be set aside, but also a deeper sensitivity and sense of positive connection emerged.

A Silent Circle

Sometimes silence is more than golden; it is a shiny mirror. A social worker in an alternative school heard a lot of shouting outside his door. It was passing time, a group of girls had gathered, and an argument broke out around boyfriends, parties, who liked whom—nothing was very clear, but everything said was very loud. The social worker stepped out and called the main cluster of girls into his office, sending everyone else off to class.

Six girls reluctantly and grumpily sat down around the room. He gave each of them a pen and pad of paper and said, "We will have a silent Circle. Please write down your thoughts as I ask these questions. Words, phrases, anything will do. What has been going on these last few weeks that has made you angry or upset?" The students wrote for a while. When it seemed most were finished, he asked, "What did you do to contribute to the problems?" Again, he waited while the students wrote. Finally, he asked them, "What can you do to make things better in the next two weeks?"

When all the girls had finished, he collected the pads. Taking each question in turn, he read to the girls what they had written. It was apparent from their responses that the girls all saw pretty much the same problems, and they were able to recognize and own up to their parts in the conflicts. The suggestions for making things better were also similar. After he read everything back to them, the girls used the talking piece to make commitments out loud to each other to listen, to not jump to conclusions, to not spread rumors, to not fight, to check out rumors before believing them, and to ask for help when they needed it from adults. The girls signed their papers and, in a much quieter manner, went back to class.

The social worker who shared this story said he knew he did not have enough time to calm the girls down by talking—they were too heated in the moment. However, by asking them to write, he gave them the means to calm themselves down and to move quickly into a process of self-reflection. Writing also helped them express their emotions without being defensive or accusatory. Everyone heard what the others had to say when they listened to the social worker reading what they had written. The process had a calming effect that helped the girls shift back into a frame of mind where they could focus on learning. It took one class period—forty-five minutes.

Middle School Sexting

Normal adolescent behavior includes flirtation and sharing secrets with the people you like, are friends with, or to whom you are attracted. But with today's technology, whispering and passing notes has become sending and receiving text messages, cell phone pictures, and videos. Teens may see this behavior as flirting, joking, or "no big deal," but adults do not always see sending photos or videos as harmless. Sending and receiving explicit pictures, even if sent to one's boyfriend or girlfriend, can be considered child pornography. It can be a felony.

A junior boy asked for "something sexy" from his sophomore girlfriend. She sent him several photos via her cell phone of herself in various states of undress. At lunch the next day, students were passing around their phones, looking at each other's pictures and videos. Two girls found the girlfriend's pictures on her boyfriend's cell phone, and laughing, sent them on to four other friends. The photos went from phone to phone. By the fifth hour, a teacher had discovered students looking at the photos and sent the cell phones down to the office. The principal handed the situation over to the school resource officer (SRO), who investigated. By the end of the day, the sheriff's office had her report, which was sent on to the county attorney. The juvenile prosecutor referred the case to a court-sponsored restorative justice Circle.

The Circle included the girl, her boyfriend, the two girls who sent the photos on, and the four students who received them—and sent them on yet again. Everyone had at least one parent with them. The assistant principal, a probation officer, the SRO, and the Circle keeper were the other adults present.

At the beginning of the Circle, all the students (and some of their parents) were angry with the girlfriend. It was her fault they were in trouble; she took the pictures in the first place. Then they listened to her dad. He said his daughter had made a poor choice in sending the pictures, but she thought it would stay with her boyfriend. She was mortified that they had gone viral and was being ostracized at school. She was thinking of changing schools and was having trouble sleeping. Gradually, everyone saw that each student had responsibility for the harm and disruption that the photos had caused and that even the initial "offender" was also a victim.

All the students agreed to write two-page essays on the dangers of sexting. They agreed to plant flowers and weed the school flowerbeds as a means of giving back to the school. The parents agreed to take the computers out of bedrooms and put them in more public places in their homes. They also agreed to block photo and video functions on their children's cell phones. The school agreed to hold a public forum for parents on sexting and technology. The county attorney did not press charges for distributing obscene materials. All the parents could look each other in the eye and smile at the end of the Circle.

Threatening Notes, Expulsion, and Circle

Perhaps the most difficult aspect of being an administrator is dealing with a student who has threatened deeply the school's sense of safety. Students who write threatening notes, bring a handgun to school, or assault another student or staff member can affect every member of the school community—including other students, staff, administrators in the building and in the district office, and every parent and family member. News stories on threats found in a school to perpetrate a school shooting, for instance, often include reports of parents deciding to keep their children home. In one instance, the investigation of a note that threatened school violence resulted in thousands of dollars of police time. In some schools, such notes lead administrators to increase police presence, install metal detectors, cancel public gatherings and assemblies, and change rules about carrying backpacks and purses.

Fear of rampage school shootings naturally colors the decisions of administrators and school boards about any threat of violence or weapons violations, especially if the weapon is a gun. Yet, though students may make threats, most do not intend to "shoot up the school." School shootings are rare, given the number of students who attend school in the United States. It is more likely that a student will be struck by lightning than be shot in a school. Even so, no administrator wants to take the chance of lightning.

Given the extremely negative impact that a gun in a school can have on the learning environment, the federal government has passed a law that requires districts to expel any student who brings a gun to school—at the discretion of the school board. Can a restorative process be used in the case of such an expulsion? Yes, and in most cases, it operates in addition to the expulsion, not in lieu of removing the student from the school district.

The following story illustrates the role that restorative justice can play in the most serious cases of potential school violence. The Circle process was used to allow representatives of the school community—from the student council president to a district administrator—to meet with the offending student and his parents. The process brought to light unexpected challenges and gifts.

Early in the school year, a ninth grader left a note threatening violence in the school. The note resulted in much disruption: the school was evacuated, police were called, an investigation was conducted, and increased security measures were put into place. But the boy was not caught. In December, he left another note. This time, after even more disruption to the school, which included media coverage and a police investigation that initially targeted students who were later proven to be innocent, he was caught. The district expelled the student from the district for an entire calendar year.

While the district policy had been followed, many issues remained unaddressed. Brittney Miller, a student reporter, described the harm that these threats had done to her:

I was sick of not being able to carry my backpack or going through metal detectors and wanted my school back. Although it seems trivial, I was also mad that the Holiday Assembly was canceled. The year continued and soon it was over. My summer, like everyone else's, was relaxing but, of course, too short. Then, I returned to school for my senior year to find myself staring back in a security camera. This brought back memories of the year before and again made me angry.

A local restorative justice program, Men as Peacemakers, was brought in to set up a Circle of accountability, as the boy and his family wanted to try to repair the harm. Brittney was asked to represent the student body in the Circle. A district administrator was invited, and the director of Men as Peacemakers attended as a concerned member of the community at large. A teacher and a police officer also attended.

In a local newspaper article on the restorative justice Circle, Brittney said, "I went in with a close-minded view that there was a bad person behind this. Fifteen minutes into it, I ended up with a box of tissues, crying."[2]

The agreement included an apology letter published in the student newsletter, which helped to explain some of the boy's motivation:

I'm the person responsible for the disruptive school days; fear of coming and outbreak of police protection starting last October of 2006. I want to apologize for this incident I caused last year. It took many privileges from the students and scared the whole community.

Having problems adjusting with the transitions at East, dealing with peer pressure and the stress it caused me, I guess I just didn't know how to handle it. The choice I made was wrong. I did something I had no intent to fulfill.

To everyone affected by this incident, I want to say I'm sorry. To the students who were accused, their privacy violated, their family life disrupted, and being [made] a victim, I apologize. To staff, police, and the community involved, sorry for the fear, headaches, chaos, and time involved.

What I did was wrong. I hurt many people in the process; I wasn't thinking. I made a bad choice; I'm not a bad person.

CHAPTER 9

Circles Inside and Outside of the School: Two Case Studies

The Circle process is a powerful tool, but Circles are not magic. They work best within a school that is intentional about addressing the needs of the whole child: academic, social, emotional, and physical. Circles can also support youths' secondary education, even while holding them accountable for crimes committed in the community.

In this chapter, I present two case studies of ongoing Circle programs. Through my position at the Minnesota Department of Education, I have developed long-standing relationships with the key individuals involved, especially Oscar Reed and Julie Marthaler. I have had the privilege of witnessing the growth of both Circle programs over several years. While I have not conducted a formal academic study of these programs, I have gained an in-depth knowledge of what these restorative justice professionals are accomplishing through their commitment to using Circles and restorative practices with youth. I have had countless conversations and correspondence with them and with many of those involved—staff, students, and youth. From notes of conversations, correspondence, and personal interviews, I can now share some remarkable work.

Case Study 1: St. Louis Park High School

For over eight years, I have invited students from the St. Louis Park High School who are members of two Circle support

Participants in the June seminar on "Restorative Measures in Schools" pose with Oscar Reed and members of Boys2Men, a St. Louis Park High School Circle, June, 2007. Photo courtesy of St. Louis Park High School (SLPHS).

groups—Boys2Men and Young Women of Divine Achievement or YODA—to describe their Circles to adult educators. The high school students' presentations about their in-school Circle program reduces skepticism about the usefulness of the Circle process and challenges some of the adults' preconceived notions about youth, race, and gender expectations. As the young men and women share their experiences and answer the educators' questions, the values and principles of the Circle come alive.

St. Louis Park is a first-ring suburb of Minneapolis. For decades, the city has had a significant Jewish population, and one can see a community menorah by City Hall in December. Mostly middle class, the voters of St. Louis Park have not missed voting for a referendum in decades to support the school district, even though currently, only 16 percent of the families in the community have children who attend school in the district. The district has an annual enrollment of about 4,300 students in kindergarten through grade twelve.

The school district has three elementary schools, a middle school, and a high school. The student population has remained steady over the past ten years due to a statewide open enrollment policy. In Minnesota, students may enroll in districts outside of the home district in which they live. In addition, suburban school districts in the Minneapolis/St. Paul metropolitan area, including St. Louis Park, agreed to a voluntary school desegregation plan formulated in the late 1990s. Besides helping to keep the enrollment strong, the desegregation plan has had the intended outcome of diversifying the district's student body. In 2011, St. Louis Park School District's population was 62 percent White, 23 percent Black (mostly African American and Somali), 8 percent Hispanic, and 6 percent Asian American.

These numbers were replicated in all the suburban districts participating in the desegregation plan. In a short time, there were more students of color, immigrant students, and students from poverty. This change challenged staff and administration to identify needs and to figure out how best to address them. Hiring translators was an obvious answer to help some students. Helping youth feel connected to a new school in a new community takes more time. Ensuring academic success is a priority, but it is not always easy to achieve.

In the early 2000s as the makeup of its student body was changing, the St. Louis Park District received two sources of extra funding: a State Incentive Grant (SIG) from the Minnesota Department of Education and special funding to aid districts with their desegregation plans. The SIG grant was designed to help a community address the use of alcohol, tobacco, and other drugs.

As a prevention program, the grant allowed the district to conduct a comprehensive needs assessment. One of the needs identified was to help all of the incoming ninth graders to establish themselves socially and academically in the high school. Another need that was identified concerned the African American students. The boys and girls were achieving at lower rates than their White counterparts. As a group, they were less likely to sign up for advanced placement courses. Their attendance was problematic. They were being referred to the principal's office at a higher rate, and they seemed to be less engaged in the life of the school.

Creating the Boys2Men (B2M) Circle

The district set up a number of programs to address these needs. One of them was to establish boys and girls groups specifically for African American students. The students were offered the chance to participate in the group through faculty and staff referrals, family referrals, or as an option that they themselves could choose.

"We wanted to hear the voices of the students and find out from them what they needed to be more successful in school," said Stacy Collins, who helped set up the programs. "But we didn't want to say to them, 'You are failing, tell us why.' Deb Zelle, the school psychologist, had worked with Oscar Reed on another issue, and she suggested that he come in and work with the boys to more organically find out what they needed."

So, St. Louis Park hired Oscar Reed to facilitate the boys' group. A former Minnesota Viking with three Super Bowl rings, Reed has been working with youth since he retired from professional football. He first founded the community agency called Life's Missing Link (now The Link), and then he developed a consulting business called the Restorative Way, which provides training and Circle keeper services to schools, community organizations, and the criminal justice system. Reed is trained in group conferencing, family group decision-making, facilitating victim-offender dialogues in crimes of severe violence, and the

The students of Boys2Men meet in the large meeting room at St. Louis Park. Photo courtesy of St. Louis Park High School (SLPHS).

Circle process. He decided to set up a Circle with the boys. He taught them the process and how to be keepers themselves. Collins also participated in the Circle as the school staff person. "It became more than a feedback group for the school," she noted, "but its own community."

"Initially, twenty boys were identified and invited to participate, but as the group started to gel, more people wanted to participate." Over the years, about twenty to thirty boys have come to meet each Tuesday. The Circle needed a name, and the students adopted "Boys2Men," soon nicknamed "B2M." They felt that this name described the process they were going through by being part of the Circle. As one student said, "'Boys2Men'—it means life. If you are a male, you are a boy coming out of the womb. As you gain in wisdom, you become a man." Another member put it this way: "It is the process of high school. You don't know what to do, don't know how to do things. This Circle teaches you honor."

The students of Boys2Men sit in Circle. Photo courtesy of St. Louis Park High School (SLPHS).

Circle values embody youth development principles. Everyone is equal in the Circle; everyone has, as Gisala Konopka wrote, "the opportunity to reflect on their behavior with peers, to engage in decision-making, and to be a part of their community."[1] As a natural part of their development, youth seek such opportunities. When adults don't provide them, they make these opportunities themselves in good or harmful ways. The Circle provided a framework in which they could establish their own values and group identity. In the Circles, they could connect with each other, as well as with caring adults and the school.

The group was formed specifically for African American boys. The segregation of a racial, gender-specific group for an hour each week raised questions among staff and students: If this is good for these boys, then why isn't it available to all students? Why are these boys being segregated? Isn't this a form of reverse discrimination, providing services to some based upon race that are not available to others?

Even though the funding for the group comes specifically

from desegregation funds—funds designed to support youth of color as they move into predominately White suburban districts—these questions were raised and are valid. The development of the group has been interesting to observe with these questions in mind.

Relationships with Teachers

Every June, the Minnesota Department of Education, in partnership with the Minnesota Restorative Services Coalition, sponsors a seminar for educators on how restorative measures are being used in schools "to improve school climate, supplement or organize classroom management approaches, prevent and address bullying, teach, and repair harm as a discipline tool." The participants "learn the principles of restorative measures and explore ways to use and adapt the practices in classrooms, in youth programming, and as part of the whole school environment."[2]

The members of Reed's Boys2Men group have been invited to speak at the seminar regularly. When they first came, they talked about not being sure what to think of the high school teachers. In their view, some teachers did not have enough time for them or were mean. Some students were wondering if the teachers were racist.

As the first year of Boys2Men Circles became the second and third years of meeting, their relationships with the teachers developed, and their remarks about the high school's staff changed:

- "I like how Mr. G gets in your face and tells you about work; he doesn't want anyone to fail."
- "The teachers give me any and every opportunity to raise my grades."
- "Some teachers are not fair, but I like Ms. B, because she explains things and then lets us talk and do our work. Some teachers, you can talk to them about other things."

As the students grew secure in their relationship with each other, they considered more options in how they interpreted the staff's behavior. When a teacher called a student out, they might have assumed at first that he or she was exhibiting racist behavior. Later on, though, they wondered instead if the teacher was just having a bad day. Coming from a place of strength with their peers, they gained confidence and a sense of greater safety in the school. The Circles gave the boys the emotional space to develop manly, adult qualities of tolerance, nuance, understanding, and respect.

The adults were also intentional in helping the students find comfort in the school. Angela Jerabek, the student assistance director for the district, set out to secure publicity for the group. "We wanted a formal mechanism to establish B2M's status. I got stories in the local paper and the *Star Tribune* [a Minneapolis-St. Paul newspaper] on a regular basis to give status to the students. There were their names in print, pictures of the students, and stories about their work, such as tutoring students in the elementary school. I tried for a story somewhere every two months."

Understanding adults is the standard work of all youth. But the Boys2Men group has also benefited from the adults who take them seriously. B2M has had standard meeting times with both of the principals who have run the school during the group's existence. Called by the B2M secretary, an elected position, the meetings provide everyone with a chance to discuss how to improve the school. The meetings are held in Circle, and that process has served the students well, even when the issues have been contentious.

"We had a staffing change with B2M," said Rob Metz, the principal. "The district staff member who supported the program and whom the boys like a lot left by mutual agreement. They were very upset about this. So, they called a meeting with me. We met in Circle. Everyone got to talk. It was the most respectful discussion over grievances ever." The co-captains meet regularly with the principal to discuss school safety, academics, and climate.

Helping Make a Safe School

Additionally, the principal and teachers look to B2M members for help in stopping fights. Collins gave an example. "B1 hallway is trouble," said Collins. Situated by the locker rooms and away from most classrooms, it was where most fights and bullying occurred. Students did not like to have their lockers in that area. "The principal asked B2M to help, and they took charge of that hallway," Collins recalled.

If there was a fight planned, B2M members invited the would-be combatants to the Circle. Besides helping the fighters by giving them a chance to say their piece, the members of the Circle would also remind them that, if they were African American, their behavior would affect all African American students in the school. "They pointed out," Collins said, "that 'this is a primarily White staff, and they can't see past you and your behavior to see me as someone else.' They would say, 'You get into a fight, and you are not helping my cause, you are ruining all our reputations.'" Of course, they also discussed that when individual White students got into a fight, they did not bear the extra burden of giving all White students a bad name. Because they were African American, they had to deal with the legacies of racism in ways that the White students did not. Reed's Circles provided profound support in helping these young men negotiate this terrain.

The Circles also provided school staff with a ready means to seek support for the African American students. Collins, for example, would serve as an advocate for the boys to the faculty. She facilitated conversations between willing teachers and students. These intentional dialogues about difficult subjects, which often involved race, gave teachers insights into behaviors that they had never before considered harmful. "For instance," Collins said, "one student told a teacher that when he gets called out in front of everyone in the class for not having his assignment done, and he is the only Black student in the classroom, that makes him feel even more of a target or an outsider than he already felt. The teacher had not considered how his behavior might negatively influence the other students' opinion of the young man, not just as a student but also as an African American student. He apologized and became more discreet in his dealings with the student."

From this conversation came policy changes. The school instituted preferential scheduling in Advanced Placement (AP) courses, so that those classes would have a cohort of Black students.

The African American students had other concerns around the legacies of racism that needed to be discussed as well. Jerabek said that the Black students thought if they asked a White peer for notes, the perception would be that they were not very good students, even though asking for notes was a common mechanism for keeping up with schoolwork. It was something that most students did. "Wouldn't it be cool," Reed mused, "if the teachers were used to Circle, and when something like that came up, they could pull the class together in Circle to talk about being or feeling different?"

"I have this vision," Reed said, "of unnecessary suspensions being a thing of the past. Kids are suspended for spitting and for raising their voice to a teacher—they get three days." The school district is moving towards making such a vision a reality. The new bullying policy includes the option of a restorative process as a discipline response. In addition, suspensions often have a restorative component. The staff are offered trainings and workshops on the Circle process. Reed fits classroom Circle requests from teachers between his regular B2M circles. "Teachers stop me in the halls and say, 'Can you help me?' I feel like I am doing Circle 24/7!"

Reed now works at the Multi-Cultural Center and runs a girls group as well as B2M. The Multi-Cultural Center's room is brightly colored. One wall is painted in a collage that incorporates the flags of many countries—one of the girls in the group designed it. The desks in the room are arranged in a circle. The room has windows and is on a main hallway. "I want this 'multi-culture room' to be a place where students can come and feel welcome," Reed said, "but also I want other people to see these kids studying—to help change public perceptions."

The perception of the students does seem to be changing in the general school culture. Jerabek said that adults have gone from talking about "those kids" to having different expectations. "When you take the ACT and score 31 [excellent, the top 98th percentile], and you are not taking AP courses, people will look at you different. These kids have exposed their hand, and there are a lot of adults who know that these kids are capable." As one boy said, "Teachers try—they don't give up even." "No teacher wants me to fail," said another. "They help me—they provide extra help, early or after school."

Youth Leadership

Although the B2M students' academics have been shaky at times, year to year, their leadership skills have grown. Because members of the Circle were able to negotiate a truce between two groups who were fixing for a fight or two and because of their effectiveness in diffusing trouble in the hallway, they are seen as assets in the school community. St. Louis Park is home to the Search Institute, which has identified forty developmental assets for youth to grow and thrive into adulthood.[3]

Perhaps the most striking bit of hard data is that the members of B2M have not been suspended for a fight since its inception. Two stories illustrate why.

In late September of 2008, a couple of boys were circling in the hallway, posturing to fight. A crowd was gathering, and an assistant principal stepped in to try to diffuse the situation. Otha, a B2M member, saw that the adult was not going to be able to stop the fight from happening, so he stepped in. "What do you want to do this for?" he asked. By the time other administrators got to the hallway, Otha was sending everyone on their way. "Go back to your offices, nothing to see here," he directed them.

The two would-be fighters were invited to the next B2M Circle to talk things through with the group. They acknowledged that the fight would have been over "stupid stuff" and not worth it.

The following February, B2M members were presenting at the Minnesota School Safety Conference in a joint appearance with the St. Louis Park Young Women of Divine Achievement or YODA (Reed had recently taken on the group in the keeper role). Otha, James, and Nick, the B2M co-captains, shared a new story. "I guess no one knows about this yet," Otha said. "It happened yesterday."

"There was this kid we have all known for a long time, since we were kids," James continued, "and he and another guy were going to fight in the school. But we told them not to, so they stopped. But then we heard that they were going to go at it again after school. So we went out to the parking lot, and we saw one of them swing at the other. We ran over there, and we stopped them."

"I saw this guy this morning," James continued, "before we came to this conference. I told him to stay calm, to not get into trouble, because he could throw away all that he has been working for and for nothing. So I think he's okay."

After this testimony, one of the girls spoke: "I want to thank James and Otha and Nick, because I did not know that had happened yesterday, but that guy is my brother and I just want to thank you for helping him."

For the co-captains, their actions were just something you do when you are responsible. "I used to be someone who would

The co-captains of all the Circles in St. Louis Park gather for a meeting with Oscar Reed. Photo courtesy of St. Louis Park High School (SLPHS).

jump into a fight," said Otha, "but now, I don't do that because I know a better way."

Coming to know a better way did take some time. Initially the students could not see how walking away from a fight would do anything but make them a "punk." Stacy Collins remembers the punk discussions. Finally, Reed told the boys that, even though he grew up in Memphis, he never got into a fight. "I always turned and ran," Reed explained. "Every time. You think I'm a punk? I was a running back in the National Football League. I am not a punk. Besides, running was good for my game."

"The boys were amazed," said Collins. "Turning away was a new idea for most—at least no one would admit that they would not get into a fight if bumped. But we gave them ideas on how to avoid fights—to act like you forgot something and turn the other way when you see someone who might provoke you, or to pretend you were going in the direction you were shoved anyway, so it does not look like a shove."

Now in their eighth year, the B2M members are showing their leadership skills in other ways. They have decided to address the continual questions from other students—"Why do you guys get to do this and we don't?" or "That group is just a Black thing"— by inviting male students of other ancestries to the Circle. This caused some difficulties with the school administration, as the grant that supports B2M was written as an African American-only, male-only group. So, the co-captains invited the principal to the Circle to talk about it. The Circle is now described as multi-cultural. "That's what you get," Reed observed, "when you expect youth to lead. They actually lead."

While the boys have taken on responsibilities, they also benefit from Reed's supportive role. He listens and then invites in resources. When some of the boys talked about not being able to stay awake in class, for example, Reed asked the school nurse to come in to talk about the benefits of breakfast and the advantages of adequate sleep.

Some young African American men see only the offender side of the criminal justice system. They may know someone who has been arrested; they see African Americans in the role of offenders in pictures, in crime stories, in the newspaper, or on the web; or they themselves may have had a brush with the law. So, Oscar asked Justice Alan Page, his former African American teammate who now sits on the Minnesota Supreme Court, to come and talk with the group. When it became difficult for Justice Page to fit these visits into his schedule, they switched venues. A trip to the state supreme court building for a meeting with Justice Page and pizza is now part of the Boys2Men's yearly schedule. Business executives, former (and reformed) gang members, and retired professional athletes have all met with the Circle. Whatever the issue, Reed tries to connect the youth to caring adults and role models.

Circle Expansion: The Multi-Cultural Room

The Boys2Men Circle is part of the St. Louis Park Student Advocacy Program. Other programs have developed to increase student achievement. These include the Young Women of Divine Achievement, a group for African American and African girls; and the Latino Association for Higher Education, set up by a graduate student working toward his masters in social work. In the Latino group, "We speak English, Spanish," said Lafredia, a student member, "or Spanglish, and we had a translator for one girl who speaks no English." The school is also forming a Muslim Student Association. In 2010, the district took in a few hundred Somali students from a nearby charter school when it closed.

All of these groups follow the model of B2M and are run in Circle. Even the HAP or High Achievement Program for grades eight to twelve, including its After-School Student Support and Tutoring Program, starts in Circle. Students check in about academics before beginning their homework. "We talk about where you are struggling and where you are excelling," said Dononda, one of the students. "Then you know who can help you. It's helped me in my classes." The Multi-Cultural Center's room is open for grades nine to twelve, and a teacher is available as a tutor each hour. Both YODA and B2M have two levels. The tenth- to twelfth-grade students are in one set of Circles, and ninth-grade students have a separate set of Circles.

YODA is as old a group as B2M, though it started out as a support group, not a Circle. The transition from support group to Circle was not easy for the girls. "YODA was kind of messy," said Chanell. "No one took it seriously; people talked out of turn." There was no agreement about confidentiality, and stories were told outside of group. The process itself was a little like a court. One student explained, "It didn't feel equal, and people saw it as a ticket out of class." "We had to raise our hand, and the captains who sat in front of us chose who could talk," explained Paris.

"Circle was so different. It taught us patience." Channel added, "Now I understand why the boys didn't trust us. Now we can sit in the boys' group and participate." Shane, a B2M co-captain, agreed. "The girls' group was not very confidential, but now it is. Their conversation is just as deep as the boys' is."

Respecting the talking piece gives form to the Circle; confidentiality provides the Circle's sense of safety. When Reed took on YODA and introduced Circle values, the girls struggled with the guidelines, especially "What is said in Circle stays in Circle" and "Respect the talking piece." Oscar asked the boys if a few girls could come to their Circle to see how things worked. Cautiously, the boys agreed, and the girls learned by watching and doing with the boys. Then, one of the YODA Circles "really opened up." "Last year," Raquel remembered, "one of the leaders opened up. She was the strong leader, and she cried, so everyone could cry, and then it was okay to open up."

YODA now has the respect of the boys. "We have seen a progression," said DeMonte. "At first, they were very chaotic and accountable only to their own person. Now they have to take into account that Circle is to be respected, and so what is talked about has not gotten out." Eli agreed. "They can come to our group (B2M) now—it's okay. They can give us perspective. They don't argue in their Circle; they don't fight; they don't walk out; there is no tension. Their program has really grown."

The administrators have noticed this growth. One session in particular illustrated the sophistication of the girls and their Circles. Upwards to sixty girls—tenth to twelfth graders—were showing up for Circle. "All we could do was a check-in," said Reed, "and then they would have to go back to class."

The six co-captains came up with a process to handle the crowd. As the girls came into the Circle room, the co-captains were at the door, directing each student to Circle A, B, or C. Then the co-captains, in teams of two, kept the Circles. The keepers all used the same questions during the Circle that they

As communication becomes more complex, the kinds of processes required to address needs for information, to problem solve, and to repair harm become more complex as well. Photo courtesy of St. Louis Park High School (SLPHS).

had developed beforehand. Reed sat on the side, with nothing to do. Pretty soon, he said, "I had to have someone else see this." He went and got the principal. Mr. Metz watched as the sixty or so girls talked quietly and listened closely to each other. "The assistant principal has to see this," Metz said. He found him and brought him to the room. The three men watched as the girls, focused, talked until the end of the period.

Boys2Men, YODA, and the other St. Louis Park High School Circle programs compliment each other. "YODA and HAP intertwine," Abrar explained. "They both help. They go hand in hand." Paris observed, "YODA helps with emotions—to get those out of the way." "What teachers don't realize," said Raquel, "is if you have a hard life at home, that affects your school life." "Yes," said Djitu, "academics, culture, personal sides all help."

Jim Radde, a community restorative justice trainer and practitioner, asked to sit in Circle with the Boys2Men group and was invited to do so. Photo courtesy of St. Louis Park High School (SLPHS).

While the support they experience from each other gives the members of the Circles a sense of responsibility and grounding, it is not an academic program. "But," said Reed, "the members are accountable to me and to each other to keep up with their classes. We can recommend them to the HAP program, for instance, and that has helped get more of these students into Advanced Placement courses."

District Evaluation

According to data collected by Stacy Collins and Shlynn Hayes, the coordinators of the St. Louis Park Student Advocacy Program, these programs are clearly helping to increase student academic achievement. Participating students improved their credit accrual from semester to semester. They failed fewer classes than their non-participating peers, and they steadily increased their passing rates. Particularly in the HAP group, which was designed to increase participation of underrepresented populations in advanced-level coursework, students went from a 93 percent passing rate in the first semester of 2006–2007 to a 100 percent passing rate in the second semester. The previous school year saw a similar improvement. In the 2005–2006 school year, the passing rate improved from 97 percent passing in the first semester to a 100 percent passing rate in the second semester.

Here is how the Boys2Men Circle is described in district publications:

> A group for African American boys in grades 9–12. It is a weekly support and advocacy group where the students meet to talk about school successes, barriers, needs, etc. It is run in a restorative justice Circle practice that teaches respectful communication and active listening. The goals of the group are to increase academic performance, social skills and support students with personal issues.[4]

Participation in Boys2Men is voluntary, but the evaluation noted a clear benefit for students who participated in the Circle 50 percent or more of the time. Among frequent participants, the passing rate went up from first to second semester by 7 percent. Seventy-seven percent of the students passed their classes in the first half of the school year, while 85 percent of the same students passed their classes in the second half. Credits awarded also increased from the first to the second semester. Over the two years that Collins and Hayes reported (2005–2007), the number of students participating in the Circle who received one or more Fs decreased from 89 percent in the 2005–2006 school year to 69 percent in the fall semester of 2006 and then to 57 percent in the spring semester of 2007.

Reed conducts Circle for boys in the Junior High School as well. The junior high Circle members also posted a decrease in the number of students who received one or more Fs: from 74 percent before they began collecting data to 67 percent after their data-collecting period.

The Higher Achievement Program was designed to give underachieving students the support and skills they need to be able to take advanced placement classes and to prepare for the SAT and ACT college entrance exams. One B2M member took the ACT preparatory classes after school and then scored a 31 (out of a possible 36) on his ACT test. "The teacher at HAP said to me, 'With a score like that, how come you are not taking AP classes?' Now they have me in these AP classes, which will help me get a scholarship to college. I never would have thought of going to college when I came to high school." Otha is currently in his sophomore year at a college in North Dakota.

Day-to-Day Circles

What do these Circles look like day to day? To start, those present are there because they want to be there. Choice is a significant element in both restorative justice and youth development theory. When young people get to choose an activity, the choice acts like a down payment. It gives them a desire to make things work, however small that desire may appear to adults. In a restorative justice process, choice is essential for safety and for the possibility of success. When young people choose to attend a Circle to repair harm, they put a part of themselves on the line. If for no other reason than to save face, they are more likely to want the process to be useful—to themselves as well as to the others.

Because of choice, the number of students attending a given Circle meeting varies. People who want to be in the Circle attend the Circle. Some students come to the Circle once or twice but then stop, often because they are not interested in keeping with Circle values. But, as the stories of the group indicate, the influence of the Circle members extends beyond the Circle itself.

The Circle opens with a handshake—one youth gets up and shakes the hand of the youth on his left, and then proceeds around the circle. The next youth stands and follows the first in shaking hands around the circle. Each youth follows suit, until everyone has shaken every one else's hand. The ritual is one that they follow with every public presentation. After the handshake, they go through their guidelines, which direct the way they operate.

On a piece of white tagboard, which can be carried easily to any room where a Circle is held, they have written the guidelines:

Speak only when you have the "TP" (talking piece).

Speak from your heart.

Honor confidentiality.

Listen with respect.

You may pass.

"Honor confidentiality" is very important for the group. A co-captain explains why. "What is said in Circle stays in Circle. You have to trust each other, or else no one will talk." "I came to get out of class," one student said, "but a co-captain opened up to the group. I saw people had the same problems as me." Another said, "It is a good place where I can tell people my problems and it [does] not get out."

"The guys get together in Circle," said Reed, "and sometimes when they go deep, my heart just falls out of my chest." "Going deep" includes talking about family issues, a desire for retaliation against someone who assaulted a sibling, concerns about alcoholism, or parental conflicts. If a member is particularly troubled, some boys will huddle up with him after Circle and talk longer. They share recommendations to keep cool and to learn from others' experiences. "The Circle helps you reach out to people and to understand and to help people," one member said.

One year, a new guideline was added: "No use of the N-word."

During Boys2Men Circle gatherings, the centerpiece and guidelines are laid out so that all participants can see them. Photo courtesy of St. Louis Park High School (SLPHS).

The story behind this guideline underscored the differences be- tween generations and the importance of being able to discuss anything in Circle. I ran into Oscar Reed at a conference. Over a hotel dinner of chicken and rice, he said he was quite bothered by "his guys." "They are using the N-word like a slang name. They say it is their right to make the word mean what they want it to, like it means 'Brother.' They don't seem to understand its power."

Reed grew up in Mississippi and Tennessee during the days of Jim Crow laws, sharecropping, and finally the civil rights era. He noted, "These guys don't know what it is like to see your grand- dad called that name by a White man. The change you see in your granddad's eyes, on his face when he hears that, you never forget. We are going to have to talk about this."

Stacy Collins remembered that discussion well. "The students really held tight to the idea that they were taking this word back and taking its power for their own. Yet, they did not know its history. They did not have that insight. The conversation was very powerful." The resulting agreement was that the word would not be used in Circle.

In addition to talking about race, racism, and the impact these were having on their lives, the students experienced growth in other areas through the Circle conversations. They talked about their relationships with their peers, especially around fighting, and with teachers. And they talked with Oscar and Stacy about language, perceptions, and generational differences. One of the most significant areas of learning for them was self-advocacy. They learned how to speak up for their needs, rights, concerns, and options in effective ways with both peers and those in authority, most of whom were White.

Influences on Family

Some of the members of B2M reported that being part of Circle had an effect on their families. Some talked about how it helped improve their communication with family members. "It helps me speak my mind more to my mom and not hide stuff," said a sophomore. Another agreed: "I learned how to be more mature, and I am better able to talk to my mom, and I can talk about something serious. I used to talk a lot, but I didn't talk about nothing."

Another member noted that it wasn't that the family changed or that he felt closer to the members in his family. Instead, the change was in him, and this shift improved the dynamics within the family. "I learned how to deal with certain types of people. I could really come together in an argument. B2M helped me learn how to deal with people and to understand people."

"I am a better listener, I think," said another, "and I can tell [my family] my problems more easily." Not all members felt an improvement at home, but all agreed that the Circle was a place they could bring trouble to and get help. "We get help from group," one tall young man said. "It's a whole family deal. I see some guys here as family. We can relate to their situation; we can offer advice. This has helped me all four years."

Academic Focus

After the Circle handshake, the B2M members do an academic and social check-in. "This focus on academics helped them to take responsibility for their own stuff," Collins reported. "They started to ask for help instead of acting up to get help." She tells the story of James, who was not doing well in math. The teacher gave tutorials after school a couple days a week, and he went to those, but he still did not do well in the class. "He admitted that he was not doing as much work on math as he could," Collins said, "so James started a math study group with his friends. His grade improved."

Keeping the academics as much of a routine as the opening handshake has proven to be a challenge, however. The 2008–2009 school year started with the Multi-Cultural Center's coordinator leaving—the third staffing change in two years. The staff change caused a drop in the academics, reported Jerabek. "We started seeing 'masking behaviors,' students saying things like, 'Oh, I didn't want to go to a four-year college anyway,' when faced with failing grades." The situation came to a head the last six weeks of the year. Several seniors were in danger of not being able to walk in graduation, and underclassmen were underperforming as well.

The adults gathered together, and they called a meeting of all the African American seniors. "We met with the students," said Metz. "Parents, staff, counselors, the athletic director. We were trying to put the pressure on them to finish strong. The students had good thoughts and suggestions."

The adults wanted the students to self-advocate—to go to the teachers to find out what they were missing, what tests needed to be made up, and what extra credit could be done. But they also wanted to provide the students with support. The staff Equity Team set up their own after-school tutoring program. The athletic director said that students could skip practice to attend tutoring without fear of not running in the meet or playing in a game. The parents shared their expectations. When one student noted that only the Black students were in the meeting, but that some White students were failing as well, a parent responded, "Don't worry about the bigger issue—worry about your own stuff."

The school's "own stuff" is something that Metz is aware of. "We are a White middle-class institution, and we have institutional racism, and we are trying to compensate for that." Jerabek added, "My concern is the social norm. When I did a 'dip stick' of failures, counting the failures at one point in time, I found that 13 percent of our White students were failing, but 60 percent of the Black students were failing a class. This is the bumpiest academic year for our African American students."

The 2008–2009 school year ended on a positive, albeit messy note. After all the interventions, meetings, Circles, and tutoring, the seniors from Boys2Men ended up graduating, either on time or in the summer. According to Carol Johnson, secretary to Principal Metz, of the thirteen eligible seniors, six students had all the credits needed for graduation in June. Five students needed one to two more credits and completed them in summer school, so that they received their diplomas before fall (they were able to "walk" in the June ceremony). One student had all his credits, but he needed to pass one of the state standardized tests, which he passed in July. Everyone who had post-secondary plans, from college to culinary school, started their post-secondary career in the fall of 2009.

The last student is a case study of mobility and the effects that moving from district to district and school to school can have on academics. This young man did not have enough credits to graduate at the end of the 2009 school year. He took classes at an alternative school and is making progress, although, as of April 2011, he still has not graduated. This student started in Minneapolis in 2004–2005, changed schools midyear, did not do well at the next school, came to St. Louis Park in 2006–2007, and was there through 2008–2009.

With Boys2Men, the adults and the students saw that the African American students at St. Louis Park High school could achieve. What they needed to establish was a strong social norm to achieve academically. Their academic norm needed to be equal in strength to their social norm to stop fights, negotiate, and support each other. "Academically, they showed their hands," Jerabek said. "We know they have the capacity."

Case Study 2: Yellow Medicine County Restorative Justice Program

Schools are not the only place where the Circles process can be applied to support youth and their education. Courts or county attorneys in some Minnesota counties have been diverting youth offenders to community Circles of accountability. The keeper, once a probation officer, is now the restorative justice coordinator for the county. The members of the Circle are community volunteers who have attended a three-day training on the Circle process. At any one time, two to three youth who have been referred to the program meet with their Circles every other week for five months to two years. During this period, they address the harms they have caused, eventually meet with their victims (if their victims want), and complete their accountability agreements. In addition, the Circles support the youth in addressing any issues that might prevent them from functioning well in the community.

Here is a description of one of these Circle programs. This restorative justice program illustrates the possibilities of Circles for holding youth accountable, for strengthening their education, and for helping them find a good path and stay on it.

Using Circles Outside of the School

Yellow Medicine County is situated in southwestern Minnesota. The prairie land with river valleys is home to towns of 300 to 3,000 people, who are served by small consolidated school districts. For the last ten years, the county has had on staff a restorative justice coordinator, who has trained volunteers to be community Circle participants. During any one month, up to five Circles may be meeting to provide care and accountability to two to three youths. The crimes they have committed span a range—theft from a church, truancy, burglary, damage to property, underage alcohol consumption, or assault. The coordinator keeps every Circle.

Yellow Medicine's (YM) Circle program started in 2001. The local mental health collaborative approached people who had a stake in the juvenile court—judges, prosecuting attorneys, probation officers, defense attorneys, school administrators, mental health staff, and law enforcement—about establishing a Circle sentencing process. Instead of punishing the youth offenders through probation and incarceration, the thought was to work with them, holding them accountable to a Circle made up of community members as well as the people affected by their actions: family members, victims, neighbors, or friends.

The stakeholders acknowledged that the traditional court process was not reducing recidivism or the soaring out-of-home placement costs. The program was developed and volunteers were recruited. An initial Circle training was held. And a handbook was written to guide the process.

Volunteer Training and Participation

A father-daughter team from Onamia, a small town north of the Metro area, along with Gwen Chandler Rhivers and Stephanie Autumn, trained the original volunteers. Their story is an illustration of the maxim "You don't do restorative justice, you live it." One of the trainers, Ali Anfinson, points out that her dad, Terry, was one of the first people to be trained in Circle sentencing when the Circle practitioners from the Yukon came to Minnesota to teach the process. "My dad took the Circle to heart, brought it into our house where we would sit—my twin sisters, my mom, my dad, and I—and talk and talk and make decisions." Sitting in Circles helped to transform the usual tensions of a teen-parent relationship. It was also practical. "When I needed a car in high school, we made the decision of whether I got a car—and what kind of car—in Circle."

Terry is a former teacher, so recommending that the Circle social compact include education activities was natural, practical, and necessary. Terry worked with youth from the Mille Lacs Band of Ojibwe. He noted, "There is a high dropout rate on the rez. We always pushed the students to go back to school to get their diploma." Terry and Ali are an example of how this court-referred process—Circles to repair harm—could also be part and parcel of education, problem solving, and family life.

The ability to solve problems, though, requires a strong seed-bed of values. The Yellow Medicine Circle Sentencing program established core values for their process, including honesty, respect, integrity, equality, and mindfulness. With these values, the Circle seeks to repair the "broken social fabric and the broken relationships within the community when a crime is committed."[5]

Many youth who commit crimes are surrounded by adults who are paid to help. But in the YM Circle, the youth are surrounded by people who give their time without compensation. The Circle participants are volunteers who care about the young people in their town and want to make a difference. This has been a surprise for the Circle applicants. "It is hard to believe how much they care about me," one young man said, to which a Circle volunteer replied, "The reward we receive is seeing how you turn out in life—we just want the best for you."

After the initial training by the Anfinsons, Julie Marthaler, the county's restorative justice coordinator, trained the community volunteers in the Circle process herself. Over the years, she has trained fifty community members. For some, being in Circle is now a part of their routine. According to an annual report, the Circle volunteers devote "roughly 2,000 hours" to the program. They seem to connect to the process, said Marthaler, to a sense of belonging and an understanding of interrelatedness. Once a volunteer called Marthaler after completing a Circle program with a youth offender that had lasted almost two years, saying, "Got anything for me? I miss Circle."

The Circle is obviously more than a new version of a bowling league or community choir. Circles provide a very structured support for youth who may be missing connection or accountability in their lives.

Support for Behavior Change

In a special edition of the professional journal *Youth and Society* (December 2001), several restorative justice thinkers and researchers discussed how restorative justice is being applied to treat youth with substance abuse issues. Much of their discussion explored the role of community in supporting youth and in holding both youth victims and offenders accountable. John Braithwaite, a professor of criminology, wrote, "Restorative justice processes have much more hope of a ritual impact that might shake a substance abuser out of drift." Professor of sociology David R. Karp and professor of government Beau Breslin speak of the "web of obligations" that includes the needs of victims, offenders, and the community. They quote an article by Gordon Bazemore (professor of criminology), Michael Dooley (correctional program specialist), and Laurey Burney Nissen (professor of social work), titled "Mobilizing Social Support and Building Relationships":

> Rehabilitation is a bigger issue than changing the attitudes, thinking and problematic behavior of offenders . . . what good is an initial change in thinking and behavior patterns if the offender's relationships with law-abiding adults and peers are weak or non-existent?[6]

Not all youthful offenders in Yellow Medicine County have substance abuse problems, but the need for behavior change is real when your behavior has gotten you in trouble with the law. And, as anyone who has tried to quit smoking or to start an exercise program knows, change is hard to do.

Amanda Sieling, the assistant county attorney and juvenile justice prosecutor in Yellow Medicine County, looks to the Circles to help youth with changing their behavior. Circles provide them with a "web of obligations" from caring people in the community. Community members watch for any "drift" in the lives of the applicants, and they support the youth in establishing relationships with law-abiding adults and peers.

The watchfulness pays off. A recent Circle graduate who had had many other kinds of interventions, including out-of-home placements, explained the power of Circle: "You guys changed my life—for real." He now is on the A honor roll at school and has returned to live in his home.

Sieling has the support of Judge Bruce W. Christopherson, who has seen the negative impact of the adversarial court process. "A win is good," said Christopherson, "win-win is better, but win-win-win is best! Having served as a trial judge more than twenty-two years, I have seen that usually when someone wins, someone else loses. However restorative justice is not such a 'zero sum' matter."

Biweekly Circles

As with many Circle programs, the Circles in Yellow Medicine County meet every other week for five months to two years. The applicants need this time to work through their reparative process. This involves identifying the harm and the people the harm has affected, meeting with their victims, repairing the harm, making restitution, and rebuilding their place in the community.

The Circles can be complex, as the interweavings of a small town take time to untangle. A victim's spouse may have to serve as a translator for a Circle participant, because not many translators are available. A restaurant owner may make her party room available for a Circle meeting. An offender may need to make amends to an entire community—a small town, a church, or a school.

The harm caused by a simple theft or the underlying issues of shoplifting can be profound. A girl may need to make things "right with God" as well as with a youth leader. A boy may need to look again at the death of a friend as the beginning of a decline that led to truancy and criminal charges. A teen may need help purchasing a dehumidifier, so that he can sleep at night, so that he can get to school on time, so that he can meet his agreements with the Circle.

Many applicants to the Circle program agree to several hours of community service, which they often complete in one or two Saturdays. But one youth met weekly with her youth minister and did one hour of restitution at a time: she cleaned the church bathrooms for a year. The girl recognized the need for slow reparation, because making change is a slow process.

Marthaler notes the difference between accountability to a

Circle and accountability to a judge. "What judge would have the time to hear all this insight from a young offender, and what judge would sentence a youth to make things right with God or to learn how to buy an appliance on time-payments?" In both instances, the Circle applicants identified what *they* needed. The youth realized that he needed to move beyond apology to moral development and support—to move beyond a simple "Yes, I will get to school" to actually figuring out the health barriers to getting there.

Supporting Education

Small towns have fewer resources and fewer people than a metropolitan area, so the Circle program depends upon everyone bringing their skills and resources to the process. In addition to the translator, an engineer meets outside of Circle to tutor a youth in algebra, which is a subject that the student was failing. Several retired teachers help English language learners with their reading homework. One Circle set up a side-tutoring Circle that met every Thursday during the school year in the back room of the local pizza restaurant, the room reserved for parties. The county picks up the cost of the drinks. Each Thursday, two volunteers show up to tutor students in anything from history to science to math.

"Education became a natural issue for the Circle members with these youth," Marthaler commented. "Rebuilding your place in the community is the place where the community Circles intersect with schools, though not always in a formal way." She said that Circle volunteers naturally want to know how the youth are doing in school. "It is a part of Circle—Circle is about community; RJ is concerned with accountability to community. If you are a teen and you are not going to school, you are not working in a good way to be part of the community. And it is just obvious: if you are in school, you are not on the street, getting into trouble."

Although many retired or current educators participate in the Yellow Medicine County Circles, they are not always the first to bring up school issues. In one Circle, a woman named Avis serves as the education "warden." She is a retired insurance agent who always asks, "How is school? What do you like? What is hard? I'd like to see attendance in your weekly report to us."

At first, one Circle tried connecting with the teachers. The youth would say, "I don't do well in math because that teacher just doesn't like me." But when community members contacted the teacher, the teacher would say, "Well, if the student worked hard and showed up, he'd get it." Finally, the Circle members said, "Just bring your homework to the pizza place, and we will help you do your homework."

In addition to regular school assignments, the Circles expect the youth to do a lot of writing: apology letters, activity journals, and reflection essays. One youth was asked to write what he wanted to be when he grew up. The boy returned with a touching story of a father fishing with his son. In the story, the "father" reflects not only on his failings and mistakes but also on his hopes for his son, because, as he says to his son at the end, "I was once like you." The youth was seeing himself in the future as a caring, responsible parent—certainly a role the community hopes he can take on one day.

Outcomes

When a youth in Yellow Medicine County appears in court for a delinquent act, anyone can request a referral to Circle, including the youth, prosecution, defense, probation, family, school, or victim. Since all of these people may have been affected by the youth's actions, they all have a reason to request Circle. In 2010, for instance, the Circle Sentencing program took applications from ten youth, providing support for them, their families, and multiple victims from multiple communities. "Of the ten youth served in 2010," reported Marthaler, "three have successfully completed, three were rejected due to concerns for safety or lack of compliance/progress on their Social Compacts, and four continue in the program to date."[7]

According to data collected for the Minnesota Department of Corrections and PACT4 Families, the local mental health collaborative, the most significant results for YMC's Circle Sentencing program are the following:

- Zero percent recidivism within one year of completion.
- One hundred percent paid of the restitution owed to victims.
- From 2002 to 2010, 90 percent reduction of out-of-home placement expenditures (a decrease in fees to the county of approximately $300,000).
- In 2010, the youth completed nearly 170 volunteer service work hours.
- Before their child entered the Circle program, 65 percent of the parents surveyed reported feeling frustrated, powerless, nervous, overwhelmed, embarrassed, ashamed, or guilty.
- After their child completed the Circle program, 97 percent of these parents felt fulfilled, supported, excited, happy, hopeful, confident, calm, grateful, and involved.
- Before entering Circle, 69 percent of the youth surveyed reported feeling angry, powerless, hated, embarrassed, ashamed, guilty, or tense.
- Upon leaving Circle, 95 percent of these youth felt fulfilled, supported, hopeful, powerful, and loved. Zero percent felt hated.
- Eighty-three percent of parents, 85 percent of youth, and 100 percent of the community members surveyed felt that the Circles were a positive experience.

Yellow Medicine County Circle member William Sturgeon as Homecoming King with Homecoming Queen Citty Cole. Photo by Stukel Photography, courtesy of Granite Falls Clarkfield Advocate Tribune.

- One hundred percent of parents and 88 percent of youth surveyed responded that the community members involved in Circle care about them a great deal. Zero percent believed that the community members did not care at all.[8]

The Yellow Medicine County Restorative Justice Circle Program expanded in 2011 with two more types of Circles: the Circle of Hope and the Family Circle. The Circle of Hope is designed to provide support and healthy connections for people after they have left chemical dependency treatment. The Family Circle works with families who are in difficult circumstances and who need support and advocacy in their own community.

Working in a small town or less populated community provides the added chance to witness outcomes over time—some good, some not. For a few years, one principal in another town outside Yellow Medicine County was able to keep track of a boy who made restitution for a fight he started in school. The boy apologized to the younger boy with whom he had fought. Then, in an assembly, he apologized to the entire high school as well. It was a hard thing that he did. Even the teachers were impressed with his courage. Unfortunately, the boy did not have stable housing or a secure family life. He bounced around from place to place and was sometimes in foster care. Eventually, the principal lost track of him. "Last I heard, he was on probation, and I don't know if he is in school."

On the other hand, Marthaler gets emails from past Circle applicants, reporting on new jobs or making the B honor roll. With the support of the Circle and his own hard work of two years, one Circle graduate was crowned Homecoming King in the fall. That next spring, Marthaler saw him walk across the stage at graduation.

CHAPTER 10

The Square within the Circle

One spring, I went to visit a charter school, Volunteers of America (VOA), situated on the edge of the west bank of the University of Minnesota. The VOA is about four blocks from the high-rise sometimes called Little Mogadishu, because it holds the largest concentration of Somali people outside of Somali's capital. Ali Musse, a restorative justice facilitator, part-time cable TV producer, and former science teacher from Somalia, runs two Circles for boys and girls at the high school once a week. I went to meet with the Tuesday afternoon Circle, a group of Somali boys and girls. They were all seniors and one was a quiet and thoughtful Oromo girl.

The students were open and welcoming. They talked easily about what their Circle was—a place where they could speak and learn about restorative justice. When they met in Circle, because of the limited space in the school, they sat around a table in the lunchroom. They did not use a talking piece but they did speak in order, always going around counterclockwise. People could pass. After an opening and first check-in round, one person would stand and talk about an issue of concern. Then the discussion would go around with the intent to hear all sides, to problem solve, and to sometimes discuss conflict or how to repair harm. The students would stand to speak, just as elders would have stood to speak in a village circle in Somalia. On this day, I was in a Circle that followed a different protocol based in a different culture. But the outcomes were so very similar.

One student spoke of using the Circle as a place where he could release feelings of anger and frustration and talk about what he could not discuss in the community. Another spoke of learning that his behavior in the halls had effects on others, not always good, and that he has since changed his behavior. He has learned that he can affect others by being calm and, by doing so, he can avoid fights. A girl talked about learning how to mediate and solve problems and about how she did that with her brothers at home. Two members of the Circle, a boy and a girl, used to "get into it." The girl said she now goes and talks to the boy. They have learned how to deal with conflict and resolve it by talking. The Circle was a place where they could talk about credits and culture, school and Somali lost boys, politics, police, and pirates.

They meet once a week, usually boys with boys and girls with girls. Many said that the Circle helped them get into less trouble and have more insight into their parents. They were just glad for a place to talk. The seniors reported that they all were graduating that June with a diploma.

These students were on my mind a week later when I spoke with a school administrator who was interested in restorative justice for her school. She wanted to know how to persuade others in the school to use restorative principles. One concern she hears a lot is that people think restorative measures take too much time.

In my view, an administrator can either invest time with students up front by using a restorative process that involves all people affected by harm, or she can dole out her time over the course of the year dealing with increasingly harmful rule violations. Big fights brew on the low flame of misunderstandings and continuous slights. Office referrals take time as well, whether the students are disciplined or not. When it comes to children, the question is not *if* you give your time, but *when*.

Better yet, an administrator can invest in peace by teaching social skills and building community. Setting aside time—even once a week in a high school or daily in an elementary class-room—for students to talk, discuss, and debate with each other, to listen, confer, and problem solve with each other seems a small investment, when the results are a safer school climate.

Deborah Prothrow-Stith, a public health professor, medi-cal doctor, professor at Harvard, and author of *Deadly Conse-quences,* studies public health responses to community violence. She lists what the community needs to provide children. "It is true that the children around us are going to get our time, our attention, our money, and our resources," she says, "one way or another."[1]

"One way or another." If we don't give our time to children in the form of safety, love, good food, education, and direction, then they take it from us through illegal activities, health costs, violence, juvenile justice resources, and lost civic engagement. In Minnesota, we pay to incarcerate youth at the rate of $70,000 a year, which is more than the cost of a year at an Ivy League col-lege. I prefer the latter to the former. It is so much more fun to go to a graduation than a funeral, a trial, or a homeless shelter.

These stakes are not an exaggeration for the young men and women at the Volunteers of America High School. In that Circle, the students were talking about the lost boys—the boys who had gone to Somalia to fight in the civil war. They talked about the murder of three adults in the neighborhood that involved two boys, both teenagers. Some of those boys will never return to their families in Little Mogadishu on the west bank of the Missis-sippi. One way or another, the children are going to get our time, our attention, our money, and our resources. This is, indeed, what children deserve from us.

A school building is usually a collection of right angles—squares and rectangles stacked on top of each other or set side by side. But a school is also the centerpiece of the community circle, and children and youth come to it from all angles, from all sides. The people who send their child to a school and the people who work in the school believe, hope, and demand that the school is a place of safety and learning.

Schools—and community centers, after-school programs, wilderness camp programs, church groups, and faith communities— can use restorative measures to help ensure that children and youth have good relationships. Using Circles and other restorative practices can help youth learn how to solve problems in a good way—even if the youth have started a fight, bullied other children, or left graffiti in the bathroom.

Across Minnesota, people within the school and outside the school have taken up the philosophy and practices of restorative measures and the Circle process. They have innovated and adapted these to fit the needs of the square (the school) or the circle (the community) in which they sit. The Indigenous Peoples of Minnesota and North America have shared their wisdom, and immigrants have brought from their homelands their relational and problem-solving practices, adding their voices and insights.

This book is intended to provide pictures and stories, ideas and theory to be discussed, challenged, slept on, tried, evaluated, and improved. I hope to have provided a deeper understanding of the challenges that go with addressing harm in schools and of helping all children access good relationships and good learning.

Restorative principles and practices provide schools with alternatives to suspension, detention, and expulsion. But the philosophy, rooted in the importance of relationships, also highlights the importance of primary prevention: building community and reaffirming relationships. The Circle process—brought forth from ancient, unbroken Indigenous wisdom—was, in our current time and society, first used as a restorative intervention. But it quickly found its school cousins in self-esteem building and social emotional learning—morning meetings, Magic Circle, class meetings, and Circle Time. The Circle underscores the importance of relationships, of knowing things of a personal nature about each other, of storytelling, sharing, and connection. It provides a simple and profound way to teach and practice relational skills—listening with respect, speaking from the heart, and taking turns. Circles have proven to be a content delivery process—a way to teach an academic subject. They are also a place to practice social skills, including the skills of problem solving, empathy, and making amends. Circles are a place to safely read the first draft of a poem, ask a question in a world language, or share the trepidation of learning fractions and integers.

Restorative measures are a practical application of youth development principles as summarized in the phrase "Nothing about us without us." Discipline, as much as any set of decisions made around children, should include the voices of the students: the person harmed, the person who did the harm, and the other students (and adults) affected by the harm. A restorative process provides the opportunity to practice decision-making in collaboration with others.

As much as humanly possible, educators, policy makers, community members, and family need to remember that a student is a child, a developing young person. Mistakes are normal and developmentally appropriate. Mistakes have resulted in a multitude of useful inventions for humanity, such as the Post-it Note and the rubber tire. It is unfair for adults to respond to a student's mistake in a way that may break a relationship or even traumatize the student. Our own fears are no excuse for harming children. We can learn to talk in a calm way and to ask honestly, wanting an answer to the question "What happened?"

Restorative measures are not magic. They involve both easy and complex communication, and they require study, practice, trial and error, review, and evaluation. They cannot replace the scope and sequence of a curriculum, the daily improvisation of a highly effective teacher, or the necessity of a healthy breakfast for learning. Social emotional learning, good nutrition and exercise, sleep, academics, and good relationships are all part of and partners in education.

Restorative measures can direct a community—inside a school, as in St. Louis Park; or outside the school, as in Yellow Medicine County—to provide the Circle that holds the children and keeps them safe.

◆ ◆ ◆ ◆

Notes

Introduction

1. "In School Behavior Intervention Grants Report to the Legislature," Minnesota Department of Children, Families and Learning, 2001. This report can be found on the Minnesota Department of Education website at http://education.state.mn.us.

2. Howard Zehr, *The Little Book of Restorative Justice* (Intercourse, PA: Good Books, 2002).

3. Belinda Hopkins, *Just Schools* (London: Jessica Kingsley Publishers, 2004), 31.

1. Harm in Schools

1. Rosalind Wiseman, *Queen Bees and Wannabees: Helping Your Daughter Survive Cliques, Gossip, Boyfriends, and Other Realities of Adolescence* (New York: Three Rivers Press, 2002), 92.

2. Cordelia Anderson, *Restorative Measures: Respecting Everyone's Ability to Resolve Problems* (St. Paul: Minnesota Department of Children Families and Learning, 1997), 1. *Restorative Measures* can be found on the Minnesota Department of Education website at http://education.state.mn.us.

3. Zehr, *Little Book of Restorative Justice*, 19.

4. Bob Costello, Joshua Wachtel, and Ted Wachtel, *The Restorative Practices Handbook for Teachers, Disciplinarians, and Administrators* (Bethlehem, PA: International Institute of Restorative Practices, 2009), 56.

5. David Finkelhor, HeatherTurner, Richard Ormrod, SherryHamby, and Kristen Kracke, "Children's Exposure to Violence: A Comprehensive National Survey," *Pediatrics* 124, no. 5 (November 2009). Retrieved 16 April 2011 from http://www.unh.edu/ccrc/pdf/CV193.pdf. Also

available from the U.S. Department of Justice, Office of Justice Programs, Office of Juvenile Justice and Delinquency Prevention (OJJDP) website for the National Survey of Children's Exposure to Violence, October 2009, http://www.ncjrs.gov/pdffiles1/ojjdp/227744.pdf, retrieved 19 April 2011.

6. Legal Rights Center, "Grant Report" (Minneapolis: Legal Rights Center, 2010).

7. "Snapshots on Minnesota Youth, 2008," Minnesota Department of Public Safety. Retrieved 18 April 2011 from http://www.ojp.state.mn.us/newsletters/Snapshots/2007-09.htm.

8. Ali Anfinson, Stephanie Autumn, C. Lehr, Nancy Riestenberg, and S. Scullin, "Disproportionate Minority Representation in Suspension and Expulsion in Minnesota Public Schools," Minnesota Department of Education. Retrieved 4 January 2011 from the website: http://education.state.mn.us/mdeprod/groups/SafeHealthy/documents/Report/017654.pdf.

9. Minnesota Department of Education website, "School Report Card: State-wide Statistics," http://education.state.mn.us/ReportCard/2009/ACGR/RCF999999000.pdf. Retrieved 28 March 2011.

10. Ibid.

11. David J. Lossen and Russell J. Skiba, "Suspended Education: Urban Middle Schools in Crisis" (Montgomery, AL: Southern Poverty Law Center, 2010). See also "Federal Policy, ESEA Reauthorization, and the School-to-Prison Pipeline," a joint position paper of the Advancement Project, the Education Law Center, Fair Test, the Forum for Education and Democracy, the Juvenile Law Center, NAACP Legal Defense and Educational Fund. December 2010. This document is available at http://www.jlc.org/images/uploads/Federal_Policy_ESEA_Reauthorization_and_the_School-to-Prison_Pipeline_-_01_18_11.pdf. Retrieved 19 April 2011.

2. Restorative Measures and Violence Prevention Education

1. Cordelia Anderson, B. Morris, and M. Robins, *Touch*, a sexual-abuse prevention play for children, 1979. For information about the script, licensing to produce the play, or the *Touch* video, contact the Illusion Theater, 528 Hennepin Avenue, Minneapolis, MN 55403; phone: (612) 338-4944; website: http://www.illusiontheater.org/.

2. James Gilligan, *Violence: Our Deadly Epidemic and Its Causes* (New York: G.P. Putnam's Sons, 1996), 110.

3. Donald Nathanson, *Shame and Pride: Affect, Sex, and the Birth of the Self* (New York: W.W. Norton and Company, 1992).

4. Brenda Morrison, *Restoring Safe School Communities: A Whole School Response to Bullying, Violence, and Alienation* (Annandale, Australia: Federation Press, 2007), 47.

5. Zehr, *The Little Book of Restorative Justice*, 10.

6. Morrison, *Restoring Safe School Communities*, 44.

7. Barbara Coloroso, *The Bully, the Bullied, and the Bystander: From Preschools to High School, How Parents and Teachers Can Help Break the Cycle of Violence* (New York: HarperCollins, 2003, updated 2008), 102.See also pages 113–14.

8. Michelle Borba, *Building Moral Intelligence: The Seven Essential Virtues That Teach Kids to Do the Right Thing* (San Francisco: Jossey-Bass Publishers, 2001).

9. Robert A. Fein, Bryan Vossekuil, William S. Pollack, Randy Borum, William Modzeleski, and Marisa Reddy, *Threat Assessment in Schools: A Guide to Managing Threatening Situations and to Creating Safe School Climates* (Washington, DC: U.S. Secret Service and U.S. Department of Education, Office of Elementary and Secondary Education, Safe and Drug Free Schools Program, and the National Threat Assessment Center, 2004), 13. The first report was released in 2002.

10. Rum River Special Education Cooperative, *Circles of Success: Connecting to the Community through Circles of Success, Building Resiliency and Preventing School Failure for Students with Disabilities* (Cambridge, MN: Rum River Special Education Cooperative, 1998). For the *Circles of Success* video, the "Procedural Manual," or for general information, contact the cooperative: http://www.cambridge.k12.mn.us/~rumriversec/

11. Robert W. Blum and Peggy Mann Rinehart, *Reducing the Risk: Connection That Makes a Difference in the Lives of Youth* (Bethesda, MD: Add Health, 1997), 7.

12. Forrest Gathercoal, *Judicious Discipline*, 6th ed. (San Francisco: Caddo Gap Press, 2001), 30.

13. Anfinson et al., *Disproportionate Minority Representation*, 6–7.

14. The Advancement Project, 2010, *Federal Policy, ESEA Reauthorization, and the School-to-Prison Pipeline*.

15. Zehr, *Little Book of Restorative Justice*, 19.

16. Lorraine Stutzman Amstutz and Judy H. Mullet, *The Little Book*

of Restorative Discipline in Schools (Intercourse, PA: Good Books, 2005), 26–28.

17. Gisela Konopka, "Requirements of Healthy Development of Adolescent Youth," *Adolescence* 8, no. 31 (Fall 1973): 20. Her article is also available online at http://www1.cyfernet.org/prog/teen/konopka.html#defined. Accessed 23 October 2010.

18. Zehr, *Little Book of Restorative Justice*, 14–18.

19. Shelley Hymel, Natalie Rocke-Henderson, Rina A. Bonanno, "Moral Disengagement: A Framework for Understanding Bullying among Adolescents," special issue, *Journal of Social Sciences*, no. 8 (2005): 1–11.

20. Zehr, *Little Book of Restorative Justice*, 14–18.

3. The Restorative School

1. Morrison, *Restoring Safe School Communities*, 106–7.

2. Ibid., 109.

3. "In School Behavior Intervention Grants Report to the Legislature," Minnesota Department of Children, Families and Learning, 2001. The report can be found on the Minnesota Department of Education website at http://education.state.mn.us.

4. "The Restorative Questions" cards can be ordered from the Inter national Institute for Restorative Practices (IIRP) website at http://www.iirp.org/books_n_videos.php.

5. Margaret Thorsborne and David Vinegrad, *Restorative Justice Pocketbook* (Victoria, Australia: Curriculum Press, 2009). For more information, see the website http://www.thorsborne.com.au/manuals.htm.

6. For information on the resources developed by Belinda Hopkins, go to Transforming Conflict website at http://www.transforming-conflict.org/index.php.

7. Information on the "See It, Say It" cards and "What to Say?" DVD and facilitator's guide can be found at the Minnesota Institute of Public Health/Minnesota Prevention Resource Center website at http://www.emprc.org/catalog/minnesota-residents/videosdvd?tid=All&tid_1=49.

8. Coloroso, *Bully, the Bullied, and the Bystander*, 103–7.

9. Linda Metcalf, *Counseling Toward Solutions: A Practical Solution-Focused Program for Working with Students, Teachers, and Parents*, 2nd ed. (San Francisco: Jossey-Bass, 2008).

10. Richard Scott, Carver Scott Educational Cooperative Project YES coordinator, interview by author, 10 August 2010.

11. Ibid.

12. Gathercoal, *Judicious Discipline*, 30.

13. Gordon R. Hodas, *Responding to Childhood Trauma: The Promise and Practice of Trauma Informed Care* (Pennsylvania Office of Mental Health and Substance Abuse Services, 2006), 40.

14. Ibid., 64.

15. Stephen L. Wessler with contributing author William Preeble, *The Respectful School: How Educators and Students Can Conquer Hate and Harassment* (Alexandria, VA: Association for Supervision and Curriculum Development, 2003), 49.

16. Jane Nelson, Lynn Lott, and H. Stephen Glenn, *Positive Discipline in the Classroom* (Rocklin, CA: Prima Publishing, 1993), 4.

17. Tricia S. Jones and Randy Compton, editors, *Kids Working It Out: Stories and Strategies for Making Peace in Our Schools* (San Francisco: Jossey-Bass, 2003), 111.

18. Ken Rigby, *Children and Bullying: How Parents and Educators Can Reduce Bullying at School* (Malden, MA: Blackwell Publishing, 2008), 192.

19. Karen Dahl, Anoka Hennepin School District Safe and Drug Free Schools Coordinator, interview by author, 14 January 2007.

20. Hopkins, *Just Schools*, 29.

4. Circles in Schools: The Basic Elements

1. John G. Neihardt, *Black Elk Speaks: Being the Life Story of a Holy Man of the Oglala Sioux* (Lincoln: University of Nebraska Press, 1932, 1979), 194–95.

2. Kay Pranis, Barry Stuart, and Mark Wedge, *Peacemaking Circles: From Crime to Community* (St. Paul: Living Justice Press, 2003), 56.

3. Minnesota Department of Education, "You're the One Who Can Make the Peace," Available online at http://www.mnssc.state.mn.us/docs/school_climate/restorative_practices/Community_Circle_Activities.pdf. Accessed 9 November 2010.

4. Marion London, *Behind the Green Glass Door*, 1993, written for the Minneapolis Public Schools. For further information, contact mjolondon@mn.rr.com.

5. Pranis, Stuart, and Wedge, *Peacemaking Circles*, 103–13.

6. Ibid., 105–6.

7. Ron and Roxanne Claassen, *Discipline That Restores: Strategies to Create Respect, Cooperation, and Responsibility in the Classroom* (Charleston, South Carolina: BookSurge Publishing, 2008), 42.

5. Components of the Circle Process

1. Kay Pranis, *The Little Book of Circle Processes* (Intercourse, PA: Good Books, 2005), 12.

2. Amstutz and Mullet, *Little Book of Restorative Discipline for Schools*, 53.

3. Ibid., 54.

4. Pranis, *Little Book of Circle Processes*, 4.

5. Cindy Skalsky, email message to author, 15 March 2006.

6. Oscar Reed, interview with author, April 2008.

7. "Two Wolves." Available online at http://www.firstpeople.us/ FP-Html-Legends/TwoWolves-Cherokee.html. Accessed 18 November 2010.

8. Pranis, *Little Book of Circle Processes*, 42.

9. The second "key principle" of "Collective narrative practice" listed on the website of the Narrative Therapy Centre of Toronto: http://www.narrativetherapycentre.com/index_files/Collective_Narrative_Practice.htm. Accessed 18 November 2010.

10. For more information on social emotional learning, go to the Collaborative on Academic and Social Emotional Learning (CASEL) website, http://www.casel.org.

11. Child Abuse Prevention and Treatment Act (CAPTA) (Jan. 1996 version), 42 U.S.C. 5101, *et seq*. For more information, see the website: http://www.smith-lawfirm.com/mandatory_reporting.htm.

12. Terry Anfinson, email message to author, 6 April 2011.

13. Cindy Skalsky, email message to author, 12 November 2007.

14. Friends Schools of Minnesota training video, 1995. For information on the video, go to the Friends School web site, http://www.fsmn.org/about, and click on "conflict resolution."

15. Alice Ierley and Carin Ivker, "Restoring School Communities: A Report on the Colorado Restorative Justice in Schools Program," Research and Practice Insert, *Voma Connections* 13 (Winter 2003); Legal

Rights Center Grantee Report, 2011. For more information, contact the Legal Rights Center at http://www.legalrightscenter.org/Default.htm

16. Friends School of Minnesota, *I-to-I Conflict Resolution Curriculum*, 1988. For information on the curriculum and DVD, go to http://www.fsmn.org/about/our-approach/conflict-resolution/i-to-i.

17. Marion London, interview with author, 20 October 2009.

18. Stephanie Autumn, email message to author, 3 April 2011.

19. Ibid.

20. Pranis, Stuart, and Wedge, *Peacemaking Circles*, 70–71.

6. Teacher Testimony

1. For further information regarding "recovery schools" in the United States, go to the Association of Recovery Schools website, http://www.recoveryschools.org/.

2. Following is Angela Wilcox's resource list for teaching writing:

Atwell, Nancie. *In the Middle: New Understandings about Writing, Reading, and Learning.* Portsmouth, NH: Boynton/Cook Publishers, 1998.

Berg, Elizabeth. *Escaping into the Open: The Art of Writing True.* HarperCollins, New York, 2000.

Bly, Carol. *The Passionate, Accurate Story: Making Your Heart's Truth into Literature.* Minneapolis: Milkweed Editions, 1998.

Christiansen, Linda. *Reading, Writing, and Rising Up: Teaching about Social Justice and the Power of the Written Word.* Milwaukee: Rethinking Schools, 2000.

Fox, John. *Finding What You Didn't Lose: Expressing Your Truth and Creativity Through Poem-Making.* New York: Putman, 1995.

Goldberg, Natalie. *Writing Down the Bones: Freeing the Writer Within.* Boston, MA: Shambhala Publications, 1986.

Padgett, Ron, ed. *The Handbook of Poetic Forms.* New York: Teachers and Writers Collaborative, 1987.

Pishop, Wendy. *Thirteen Ways of Looking for a Poem: A Guide to Writing Poetry.* New York: Addison Wesley Longman, 2000.

Wooldridge, Susan. *Poemcrazy: Freeing Your Life With Words.* New York: Clarkson, Potter, 1996.

3. Linda Christiansen, *Reading, Writing, and Rising Up: Teaching*

about Social Justice and the Power of the Written Word (Milwaukee: Rethinking Schools, 2000).

4. Rosanne Bane, "If You Don't Get What You Want: Tips for Getting the Feedback You Need," *Writers Connection* (March 1997): 1, 12–13. Available online at http://www.rosannebane.com/pdf/If%20You%20Can't%20Get%20What%20You%20Want.pdf. Retrieved 23 April 2011.

7. Teaching with Intention

1. Dan Clark, *Puppies for Sale and Other Inspirational Tales: A "Litter" of Stories and Anecdotes That Hug the Heart and Snuggle the Soul* (Deerfield Beach, FL: Health Communications, 1997).

2. "In School Behavior Intervention Grants Report to the Legislature," Minnesota Department of Children, Families and Learning, 2001. This report can be found on the Minnesota Department of Education website at http://education.state.mn.us.

3. "Restorative Schools Grant Executive Summary," Minnesota Department of Education, 2003. This report can be found on the Minnesota Department of Education Website at http://education.state.mn.us.

4. For more information on SEAD, see Cordelia Anderson's website, http://www.cordeliaanderson.com/.

5. See the Minnesota Department of Education's website, http://education.state.mn.us/mdeprod/groups/SafeHealthy/documents/Report/001735.pdf.

6. See Cordelia Anderson's website, http://www.cordeliaanderson.com/.

7. See Free Spirit Publishing's website: http://www.freespirit.com/.

8. For more information on Restorative Guides, see the South St. Paul Restorative Justice Council website: http://ssprj.org/.

8. Using Circles to Repair Harm

1. Konopka, "Requirements of Healthy Development of Adolescent Youth," 20.

2. Sarah Horner, *Duluth News Tribune*, Vol. 136, No.199, 2006.

9. Circles Inside and Outside of the School

1. Konopka, "Requirements of Healthy Development of Adolescent Youth," 20.

2. From the Minnesota Department of Education website, http://education.state.mn.us/MDE/About_MDE/News_Center/013578. Accessed 29 December 2010.

3. See the Search Institute's website for more information on the forty developmental assets they have identified: http://www.searchinstitute.org/developmental-assets. Accessed 25 April 2010.

4. Collins and Hayes, presentation to the SLP School Board, 2007. For more information regarding the St. Louis Park High School's Multicultural Center, contact Angela Jerabek, counselor/grant writer, at Jerabek.Angela@slpschools.org.

5. Julie Marthaler, Yellow Medicine County Circle Sentencing Program Summary, 2010. Sent via email 20 April 2011. Contactjulie.marthaler@co.ym.mn.gov.

6. Gordon Bazemore, Michael Dooley, and Laura Burney Nissen, "Mobilizing Social Support and Building Relationships: Broadening Correctional and Rehabilitative Agendas," *Corrections Management Quarterly* 4, no. 4 (Fall 2000): 18.

7. Marthaler, Yellow Medicine County Circle Sentencing Program Summary, 2010.

8. Ibid.

10. The Square within the Circle

1. Deborah Prothrow-Stith, "The Importance of a Community Response to Violence," *Smith College Studies in Social Work* 71, no. 2 (2001): 297–304.

Resources

Organizations in the United States

Barron County (Wisconsin) Restorative Justice Programs, Inc.
(http://www.bcrjp.org/school_init.html). Click on "Practices in
School Communities."

Center for Restorative Justice and Peacemaking (http://www.cehd.
umn.edu/ssw/rjp/default.asp) at the University of Minnesota is an
international resource center that supports restorative dialogue,
practice, research, and training.

Conflict Transformation Program (www.emu.edu/ctp/) was established in 1994 at Eastern Mennonite University. The program supports the personal and professional development of individuals
as peace builders and strengthens the peace building capacities of
the institutions they serve.

Discipline That Restores (http://disciplinethatrestores.org/) is an activity of the **Fresno Pacific University Center for Peacemaking
and Conflict Studies** (http://peace.fresno.edu/rjp/) that explores
restorative discipline in schools.

Life Trax Training Program (www.csmp.org) provides mediation and restorative justice resources and training for Colorado
schools, including the video *Making Things Right: Restorative
Justice in School Communities.*

Living Justice Press (http://www.livingjusticepress.org/) publishes
books on restorative practices, especially the peacemaking Circle
process. Their website has a section called "All Things Circle" with
extensive resources about the Circle process. Another section
called "Who You Can Talk with about Circles" includes an international contact list of Circle practitioners, which is continually
growing.

Minnesota Department of Corrections, "Restorative Justice" (http://www.doc.state.mn.us/rj/Default.htm).

Minnesota Department of Education (http://education.state. mn.us). Click on "Safe and Healthy Learners." Also "Restorative Measures: Respecting Everyone's Ability to Resolve Problems." (http://education.state.mn.us/MDE/groups/safehealthy/ documents/report/002552.pdf).

Minnesota Restorative Services Coalition (MRSC) (http://www. mnmrsc.org/). MRSC is a statewide coalition to promote restorative philosophy and quality restorative services for individuals, communities, and organizations.

Restorative Justice Online (www.restorativejustice.org). This site offers a thorough introduction to restorative justice, as well as resources, research access, a "meet the leaders" page, and conference listings.

Restorative Measures in the Schools (http://restorative.tripod. com/) explains the Circle process and its use in classrooms as an alternative to suspensions. These Circle applications include the repair of harm, group problem solving, and community building.

St. Croix Valley Restorative Justice Project (www.scvrjp.org) provides victim impact panels, underage consumption panels, victim-offender conferencing, Circles, victim empathy seminars, and restorative justice in schools.

International Organizations

International Institute on Restorative Practices (IIRP), (http:// www.restorativepractices.org/) is a nonprofit organization that provides education and research in support of the development of restorative practices. SaferSanerSchools (www.safersanerschools. org) helps educators improve classroom management, school discipline, and school climate through restorative practices. The IIRP is based in Bethlehem, Pennsylvania.

Margaret Thorsborne and Associates (http://www.thorsborne.com. au/) offers services in "Transforming Conflict within Organisations," which includes providing technical assistance and training internationally on restorative practices in the workplace and in schools. Educational tools are listed under the section "Schools." Thorsborne is based in Australia.

National Center for Restorative Approaches in Youth Settings (www.transformingconflict.org) provides training, advice, consultancy, plenary speakers, workshop leaders, and partnership and educational resources, as well as training manuals, posters, and DVDs. The National Center operates in the United Kingdom.

Victim Offender Mediation Association (VOMA) (http://www.voma.org/) supports people and communities working at restorative models of justice. VOMA provides resources, training, and technical assistance in victim-offender mediation, conferencing, Circles, and related restorative justice practices.

YOUCAN (http://www.youcan.ca) is a Canadian organization focused on youth-led initiatives, and it offers a high school curriculum on the Circle process. Click on "YouCan Programs, Training."

Books

Bintliff, Amy Vatne. *Re-engaging Disconnected Youth: Transformative Learning through Restorative and Social Justice Education.* New York: Peter Lang Publishing, 2011. Website: http://amyvatnebintliff.com/Amy_Vatne_Bintliff/Home.html.

Borba, Michelle. *Building Moral Intelligence: The Seven Essential Virtues That Teach Kids to Do the Right Thing.* San Francisco: Jossey-Bass Publishers, 2001.

Boyes-Watson, Carolyn. *Peacemaking Circles and Urban Youth: Bringing Justice Home.* St. Paul: Living Justice Press, 2008. Website: www.livingjusticepress.org.

Claassen, Ron and Roxanne. *Discipline That Restores: Strategies to Create Respect, Cooperation, and Responsibility in the Classroom.* Charleston, SC: BookSurge Publishing, 2008. Website: http://disciplinethatrestores.org/. The book comes with a book study guide. Contact Ron Claassen, Fresno Pacific University, Director, Center for Peacemaking and Conflict Studies. Phone: (559) 453-3420. Email rlclaass@fresno.edu. Website: www.peace.fresno.edu/.

Hopkins, Belinda. *Just Schools: A Whole School Approach to Restorative Justice.* London: Jessica Kingsley Publishers, 2004. Website: http://www.transformingconflict.org/resources.html.

International Institute on Restorative Practices (IIRP) has published

both literature and DVDs that support restorative practices
in schools, including: *Restorative Circles in Schools: Building
Community and Enhancing Learning; The Restorative Practices
Handbook for Teachers, Disciplinarians, and Administrators;
Safer, Saner Schools: Restorative Practices in Education; Beyond
Zero Tolerance: Restorative Practices in Schools* (DVD); and *The
Transformation of West Philadelphia High School* (DVD). Website:
http://www.restorativepractices.org/ or www.iirp.org.

Mikaelsen, Ben. *Touching Spirit Bear*. New York: HarperCollins,
2002. Website: http://www.benmikaelsen.com/index.html

Morrison, Brenda. *Restoring Safe School Communities: A Whole
School Response to Bullying Violence and Alienation*. Annandale,
Australia: Federation Press, 2007. Website: www.federationpress.
com.au.

Pranis, Kay, Barry Stuart, and Mark Wedge. *Peacemaking Circles:
From Crime to Community*. St. Paul: Living Justice Press, 2003.
Website: www.livingjusticepress.org

Thorsborne, Margaret, and David Vinegrad. *Restorative Justice
Pocketbook: How to Resolve Disciplinary Matters by Enabling
Those Involved to Repair the Harm Done to People and Rela-
tionships*. Alresford, Hants, UK: Teachers' Pocketbooks, 2009.
Website: www.teacherspocketbook.co.uk.

———. *Restorative Practices in Schools: Rethinking Behaviour Management*. Training Manual. This and the following training
manual are available from Thorsborne and Associates Website:
http://www.thorsborne.com.au/. Click on "Resources, Training
manuals."

———. *Restorative Practices and Bullying: Rethinking Behaviour
Management*. Training Manual.

Zehr, Howard, Kay Pranis, Lorraine Stutzman Amstutz, Judy H.
Mullet, and others. *The Little Books of Restorative Justice and
Peacemaking Series*. Intercourse, PA: Good Books. Website:
www.goodbks.com.

This list is not exhaustive, and new resources are published regularly.
For other national and international resources, use a Web search en-
gine, with key words *restorative justice in schools, restorative practices,*
and *restorative measures.*

Index

repairing broken social fabric, 204; for repairing harm, 3, 7, 18, 49, 69, 71, 111, 163, 166, 207; and rule of three, 111; and seeing everyone, 74, 76, 112–13, 127–8, 142–43; for seminars, 163; and sentencing, 117, 203–204, 209–10; shape of, 74–75, 112–13; and side conversations, 112–13; silent, 170; of success, 38; and talking piece, 5, 75–82; and teaching, 104, 119, 125–46, 153, 157, 163, 165, 217; for transitions, 147; and values, 6, 18, 38, 74–75, 77, 80, 84–85, 87–89, 96, 109, 119, 121–22, 160–61, 168, 178, 182, 196, 204; and volunteers, 159, 203–205, 213, 215; and writing, 209. *See also* Circle applicants, Circle keeper(s), Circle questions, Circle training, consensus, stories, storytelling.

Circle training, 57, 105, 160; for criminal justice personnel, 180, 204; for keepers, 166–67; for mediators, 157; for school staff, 128, 159, 186; for teachers, 49–50, 63, 65, 95, 123, 125, 159, 180; for volunteers, 202–205

Claassen, Ron and Roxanne, 92

closing the Circle, 88, 99, 101

Cohen, Richard, 68

Collaborative on Academic, Social and Emotional Learning (CASEL), 103

collaborative problem-solving, 5–6, 13, 49, 57, 64–65, 67, 70, 118–19, 140, 204, 216–17

Collins, Stacy, 180, 189, 194, 198

Coloroso, Barbara, 33, 60,

common agreements, 77, 87, 89–91, 122

communication: face to face, 6; with family, 199; process of, 76–77, 114, 116, 119, 161; skills for, 160; and tone of voice, 57, 61

community: accountability to, 202, 208; as affected by harm, 13; and building, 3, 22, 77, 85, 104, 121, 128, 157, 214, 216; of learners, 77; as support to victims and offenders, 43, 203, 205–207, 209

community Circles of accountability, 175, 202

community policing, 54

community service, 35–36, 46–47, 207

conference, 4, 50, 118; and family, 30–32; and restorative, 28, 30, 34–35, 42, 44–46, 54, 68, 70–71, 188

confidentiality, 77, 88–89, 92, 105–108, 116, 172, 197; violations of, 191–92

conflict(s), 121, 162–63, 166, 171; addressing, 69, 157; dealing with, 49, 74, 98, 214; parental, 197

conflict Circles, 69, 164

conflict management, 67, 104

conflict resolution process, 50, 66, 68, 118

connectedness, 37, 89, 141; with family, 39; with school, 39

consensus, 38, 42, 71, 75, 77, 93, 114–16

consequences: compared with restorative approach, 5–6, 30–31, 35–36, 38–39, 41–42, 45–46, 60, 68, 116, 203; and punishment, 11–12, 60; unfairness of, 11, 23

context of harm, 9, 13, 18, 32; and culture and race, 12

control, 25, 68; and abuse, 33; over
actions, 101; and Circles, 96,
112–13; and hall standing, 55;
of impulses, 45; and keepers,
96; of nonverbal expression,
61; reframing, 64; and self-, 79,
145; and talking piece, 79
conversations, 6, 57, 108, 185, 199;
caring conversations, 106; and
problem-solving, 65; on the
side, 112–13, 143; videos with
examples of, 60
corn rows/hair braiding, 9, 11
Costello, Bob, 18
Counseling Toward Solutions
(Metcalf), 63
court process, 114, 202–203
creative arts, 126, 169
crime(s): children's exposure to,
18–19; and Circle response to,
166, 177, 203–204; livability,
54; restorative justice view of,
12; and shame, 29; victim of,
43; as violation of people and
relationships, 5, 13; and violence, 29
criminal justice system (U.S.), 18,
20; in Minnesota, 117, 180, 190
culture differences, 15, 99; and eye
contact, 83, 85–86
culture: of school, 37, 187; in the
classroom, 121, 133
cyber-bullying, 16

Dahl, Karen, 69
Dakota, 98, 122
dancing, 168–69
dating violence, 66–67
Deadly Consequences (Prothrow-
Stith), 215
death, 16, 103, 163, 207
decision-making, 42, 47, 104, 114,
138, 160; as brain function, 154;

as collaborative, 217; and family group, 180
Denborough, David, 103
desegregation, 179, 183
detentions, 23, 30, 40, 216
dialogue, 50, 58, 87; Circles for, 50,
58, 92, 150–152
difficult conversations, 60–63, 185
discipline, 3, 29, 39–42, 77–78;
by exclusion, 39–40; that
includes all voices, 217; and
learning environment, 13; and
other interventions, 22; as
reconnecting, 47; restorative
approach to, 40–43, 183, 186;
and rules, 12; as a teachable
moment, 6–7; and using Circles, 3; and "zero-tolerance"
policies, 20
Discipline That Restores (Claassen), 92–93
disclosures, 108–109
disorderly conduct, 168–69
disproportionate minority representation: in non-graduation,
21; in prisons, 20; in suspensions and expulsions, 20, 179
disrespectful behavior, 16, 55,
61–63, 65, 146, 151, 155
district policies: to desegregate,
179; for evaluation, 194–96;
and funding, 179; to get grants
for Circles, 38; about guns,
174; about mediation, 69; for
prevention programs, 3, 118,
179–80; around punishment,
11; and restorative justice,
158–60, 174–76; as rules, 12, 16;
about suspensions, 186; about
teachers standing in halls during passing time, 55–56; after
trauma, 22; around "zero-tolerance," 20–21

About Living Justice Press

A 501(c)(3) tax-exempt, nonprofit publisher on restorative justice

Living Justice Press (LJP) publishes books about social justice and community healing. We focus specifically on restorative justice and peacemaking, and within this field, we concentrate our work in three areas.

First, we publish books that deepen the understanding and use of peacemaking Circles. Circles help people deal with conflicts and harms in ways that promote justice and "being in a good way" as a way of life.

Second, because restorative justice draws directly from Indigenous philosophies and practices, we publish on Indigenous ways of understanding and practicing justice.

Third, we publish the voices of those "in struggle" for justice. Our books seek to apply what we have learned about healing harms between people to the larger and more systemic challenges of addressing harms between peoples. Through our publishing, we join in working toward justice between peoples through paths of education, exploring how to rectify harms, and transforming our ways of being together. According to restorative justice, this journey begins with hearing the stories—especially from those whose voices have not been heard—and finding out from those who suffered what it would take to "put things right."

As a community-based publisher, LJP's Web site provides not only extensive free information about restorative justice and Circles but also a national and international listing of Circle practitioners. We want to facilitate people finding Circle keepers and trainers in their areas. Our Web site also offers video clips of people who are deeply engaged in the Circle work speaking candidly about their work.

We want to thank all those who support Living Justice Press by buying our books, using them for classes, making financial donations, as well as donating time through volunteer work. We want to express our special thanks to Cathy Broberg, Dave Spohn, and Wendy Holdman for their most skilled and generous work on our behalf, enabling us to produce books of such consistently high quality inside and out. We continue to exist through the support of everyone in the Living Justice Press community. We are deeply grateful.

Books from Living Justice Press

New: eBooks!

As of June 2011, all Living Justice Press books are available both as physical books and as eBooks (ePub and Kindle formats). Our eBooks are available through either Google eBooks or amazon.com. Our physical books are available through our Living Justice Press Web site, amazon.com, or by special order through most any bookstore.

On the Circle Process and Its Uses

Peacemaking Circles: From Crime to Community by Kay Pranis, Barry Stuart, and Mark Wedge, ISBN 0-9721886-0-6, paperback, 271 pages, index; eBook ISBN: 978-1-937141-01-1.

Building a Home for the Heart: Using Metaphors in Value-Centered Circles by Pat Thalhuber, B.V.M., and Susan Thompson, foreword by Kay Pranis, illustrated by Loretta Draths, ISBN 978-0-9721886-3-0, paperback, 224 pages, index; eBook ISBN: 978-1-937141-04-2.

Peacemaking Circles and Urban Youth: Bringing Justice Home by Carolyn Boyes-Watson, ISBN 978-0-9721886-4-7, paperback, 296 pages, index; eBook ISBN: 978-1-937141-05-9.

Doing Democracy with Circles: Engaging Communities in Public Planning by Jennifer Ball, Wayne Caldwell, and Kay Pranis, ISBN 978-0-9721886-6-1, paperback, 208 pages, index; eBook ISBN: 978-1-937141-07-3.

Circle in the Square: Building Community and Repairing Harm in School by Nancy Riestenberg, ISBN 978-0-9721886-7-8, paperback, 192 pages, index; eBook ISBN: 978-1-937141-08-0.

On Indigenous Justice

Justice As Healing: Indigenous Ways, edited by Wanda D. McCaslin,
ISBN 0-9721886-1-4, paperback, 459 pages, index; eBook ISBN:
978-1-937141-02-8.

On Addressing Harms between Peoples

*In the Footsteps of Our Ancestors: The Dakota Commemorative
Marches of the 21st Century,* edited by Waziyatawin Angela
Wilson, ISBN 0-9721886-2-2, oversize paperback, 316 pages,
over 100 photographs, color photo insert, index; eBook ISBN:
978-1-937141-03-5.
*What Does Justice Look Like? The Struggle for Liberation in Dakota
Homeland* by Waziyatawin, ISBN 0-9721886-5-7, paperback, 200
pages, index; eBook ISBN: 978-1-937141-06-6.
He Sapa Woihanble: Black Hills Dream, edited by Craig Howe, Lydia
Whirlwind Soldier, and Lanniko L. Lee, ISBN 978-0-9721886-9-2,
paperback, 240 pages, index; eBook ISBN: 978-1-937141-09-7.

We offer a 20% discount on orders of 10 books or more. We are de-
lighted to receive orders that come directly to us or through our Web
site. Our books are also available through amazon.com, and they can
be special ordered from most bookstores. Our eBooks are available
from amazon.com and Google eBooks. Please check our Web site for
announcements of new LJP books.

Order by phone, fax, mail, or online at:
2093 Juliet Avenue, St. Paul, MN 55105
Tel. (651) 695-1008 • Fax. (651) 695-8564
E-mail: ljpress@aol.com
Web site: www.livingjusticepress.org

About the Author

Nancy Riestenberg has over twenty-five years of experience in the fields of violence prevention education, child sexual abuse prevention, and restorative measures in schools. She has worked with school districts in Minnesota and twenty other states, from the Cass Lake-Bena School District in Minnesota to Chicago Public Schools. She also speaks nationally on restorative measures at conferences and through trainings. She provides technical assistance on violence and bullying prevention, school connectedness, school climate, dropout prevention, cultural relevance in prevention education, crisis prevention and recovery, and restorative measures. She has also provided technical assistance in restoring the learning environment to the Minnesota school districts that experienced school shooting incidents.

Nancy was a member of the design team for the National Institute of Corrections' restorative conferencing curriculum for law enforcement and school personnel, *Facilitating Restorative Group Conferences.* She participated in the "Restorative Justice and Teen Court Focus Group" for the American Probation and Parole Association (APPA) and has written several articles on restorative measures in schools. She presented on Minnesota Restorative Practices at the *Restorative Approaches to Conflict in Schools Seminar* at the University of Edinburgh.

At the Minnesota Department of Education, she has worked

with her colleagues on evaluating and implementing restorative measures in schools. She has analyzed data regarding disproportionate minority representation in suspensions and expulsions, student survey data regarding bullying, and data surrounding the state-wide violence prevention mass media campaign, *You're The One Who Can Make The Peace.*

Prior to coming to the Minnesota Department of Education, Nancy worked for twelve years with the Illusion Theater's Sexual Abuse Prevention Program, which created and toured educational plays on child sexual abuse, domestic violence, and HIV/AIDS prevention education. She coordinated the adaptation of *Touch,* the child sexual abuse prevention play, for the Red Lake People, and trained high school students in twenty different school districts in eight states to present social-issue prevention plays to their peers.

Nancy can be reached by email at na.riese@gmail.com.

Continued from page ii

I have been anxiously awaiting this book, as I train school personnel around the US and Canada and know the great need for it. Nancy draws on her extensive experience of working with many different schools for over fourteen years. She helps them incorporate restorative approaches to discipline as well as create a healthy classroom climate. Her work offers us hope that it is possible to create schools built on respect and order without excluding those who have the greatest need for education. This book establishes why a restorative approach is important, and it is full of practical examples of how to implement it. School folks urgently need the inspiration and information in this book. Thanks to Nancy and all the pioneers whose work she shares!

— Kay Pranis, international Circle trainer and coauthor of
Peacemaking Circles: From Crime to Community

Nancy writes so clearly—she carries the reader along in a way that is both persuasive and compelling. I found myself reading line after line and thinking, 'Yes! Yes!' and then searching for a pen to record the phrases I'd like to pass on to others in my own courses and presentations—with due credit given, of course.

I love the way the book is full of stories. Restorative practice really is all about 're-storying,' giving us back the opportunity to share our own stories in any given incident, and Nancy has reminded me of the power of story to reach out to people's hearts.

But we also need to connect with people's minds, and Nancy does that too. She sets the context for her work in Minnesota—and by extension elsewhere, because I found myself making comparisons with the situation here in the UK as well. The facts and statistics she has gathered speak for themselves and help to make the case for doing differently. Nancy also reaches out to the mind with her profound grasp of the theoretical underpinnings to restorative practice, the clarity with which she explains these, and how she relates them to effective practice. Nancy, I wish I were there to raise a glass with you to toast this fabulous book. I hope it is as widely read as it deserves to be, for if it is, I think it will have a huge impact on the lives of adults and young people, not only in Minnesota schools but also far beyond.

— Belinda Hopkins, author of *Just Schools* and *The Restorative Classroom*